T[he]

Past and Present.

Gleanings

in

Local History.

By

Dugald Mitchell, M.B.C.M.

DUMBARTON:

BENNETT & THOMSON, 16 AND 18 HIGH STREET

1886.

British Library Cataloguing in Publication Data
A catalogue record of this book is available from the British Library

ISBN 1 899863 13 3

First published 1886

© House of Lochar 1996

Printed in Great Britain
by SRP Ltd, Exeter
for House of Lochar
Isle of Colonsay, Argyll PA61 7YR

CONTENTS.

CHAPTER I.
EARLY GLIMPSES.

CHAPTER II.
TARBERT IN THE FOURTEENTH CENTURY.

CHAPTER III.
ROYAL VISITS AND ROYAL GRANTS.

CHAPTER IV.
A FREEBOOTER OF THE OLDEN TIMES.

CHAPTER V.
THE SHERIFFDOM OF TARBERT.

CHAPTER VI.
MILITARY AFFAIRS, 1600-1745.

CHAPTER VII.
LAIRDS OF TARBERT: THE M'ALISTERS AND CAMPBELLS.

CHAPTER VIII.
TARBERT IN RECENT TIMES.

CHAPTER IX.
TRAWLERS AND TRAWLING.

CHAPTER X.
TALKS AND WALKS.

INDEX.

Abhuinn-nan-Ghillean, legend of, 134.

Ailean-nan-Sop, 40 ; early history, 41 ; residence in Tarbert
    Castle, 42 ; forays, 43; death, 44.

Angus Og of the Isles (1306), 11.

Angus of Islay (1263), 8.

Ardkinglas. See Campbell.

Argyll, Earl of, keeper of Tarbert Castle, 36 ; bailie and
    governor of royal lands in Knapdale, 36; sheriff of
    Tarbert, 46 ; at Tarbert (1615), 56 ; at Tarbert Castle
    (1685), 63 ; receives grant of Kintyre, 54.

Argyll, Duke of, institutes law-suit as to Castle (1762) 79 ;
    connected with Argyll Canal Company (1882), 145.

Argyll, Sheriff of, contributes to building of Tarbert Castle,
    25.

Arran, Rector of, contributes to Tarbert Castle, 25.

Artillery, Castle provided with 33.

Athole, Bailie of, contributes to Tarbert Castle, 25.

Athole, Marquis of, 62, 75.

Auchinbreck. See Campbell.

Bakehouse, 21.

Barbour's " Brus," Extract from, 14.

Barony of Tarbert, 36.

Bran, cost of watching, 22.

Brewhouse, 17, 21.

Bruce, Robert, at Tarbert (1306), 11 ; crosses isthmus (1315),
    13 ; builds Tarbert Castle (1325), 16 ; visits Tarbert
    (1325, 1326, and 1329), 18, 18, 26.

INDEX—*continued.*

Burgh of Tarbert existing in Bruce's reign, 29 ; cocket seal, 28 ; taxation, 29.

Cairnbaan, Fort near, 16.
Campbell, Dugald, Sheriff of Argyll and Bailie of Athole, 25.
Campbell, James C., Bishop of Bangor 89.
Campbell, Lieutenant-Colonel John, 86.
Campbell of Ardkinglas, 49, 54.
Campbell of Auchinbreck, 49, 54, 65, 68, 75.
Campbell of Kilberry, 56, 75.
Campbell of Kintarbert, 79.
Campbells of Stonefield, genealogy, 83 ; Archibald, Sheriff of Argyll and Bute, 84 ; John, Lord Stonefield, 85 ; Colonel Colin (younger), 86 ; John, 86 ; Colin George, 89 ; John (younger), 98. Derivation of their title, 83.
Canal, proposed, at Tarbert, 141.
Cardross, 22, 24, 26.
Carlyle's description of Haco's journey at Tarbert, 6.
Carpenter, wages of, 23.
Castle of Tarbert, built by Bruce (1325), 16 ; resided in by Bruce (1326 and 1329), 18, 26 ; visited by Bishop Lamberton and Sir James Douglas (1326), 18 ; resided in by Earl of Moray (1335), 27 ; repaired and provided with artillery (1494), 33 ; residence of James IV. (1494), 33; visited by James IV. (1498 and 1499), 34, 35; keeping entrusted to Argyll (1499), 36 ; held by Ailean-nan-Sop, 42 ; held by M'Alisters (1580), 73 ; garrisoned by Roundheads (1652), 59 ; captured by the Highlanders (1652), 59 ; the rendezvous of Earl of Argyll (1685), 63 ; subject of a law-suit (1762), 79 ; Probability of a castle older than 1325, 16. Three forts formerly guarded the isthmus, 16. Description of buildings, 18.
Chapel at Tarbert (1326), 21 ; donation by James IV., 34 ; probability of a chapel at Glenakil, 95.
Chaplain's salary (1326), 23.
Cheese, a chief article of diet in Bruce's reign, 24 ; cost of cheese, 24.
Cloth bought at Tarbert (1326), 22.
Cocket seal of Tarbert burgh, 28.
Coll Ciotach reconnoitres at West Tarbert (1615), 56 ; sur-

renders forts in Islay, 57.
Coll, Lord of, captured by Ailean-nan-Sop, 43.
Constable of Tarbert's Account (1326), 19.
Court-house, 92.
Custom, Great, 28.

De Lany, John, constable of Tarbert (1326), 19 ; his account,
     19 ; his pay, 24.
Distillery, 136.
Douglas, Sir James, at Tarbert (1326), 18.
Drinksilver given to the gunners by James IV., 34.
Dumblane, Bishop of, contributes to " bigin of Tarbert," 34.
Dundee's (Viscount) proposed march to Tarbert, 69.

Ecclesiastical affairs of Tarbert, 95.
Eilean-da-Ghallagan, 136.
Emporium for royal shipping, Tarbert an, 33
Exchequer at Tarbert, 19.

Fairs and markets at Tarbert established (1705), 77 ; descrip-
     tion, 99.
Ferry of Tarbert, 52.
Feu-charter, law-suit as to (1762), 79.
Fishing life in Tarbert, 102.   See also herring fishery.
Fool, the Court, at Tarbert, 26.
Forts.   See Castle and Eilean-da-Ghallagan.

Geographical position of Tarbert, 94.
Glenakil, burying place at, 133 ; probably the site of a
     Chapel, 95.
Glossary, 148.
Goldsmith's house, 21.

Haco of Norway crosses the isthmus of Tarbert (1263), 6.
Hall of Castle, 21.   Good Templar's Hall, 98.
Harbour dues, 106; harbour works, 90; extent of harbour, 92.
Herring fishery.   Tarbert " the capital of herringdom," 102.
          Mode of fishing, 103, 108.   Large hauls of herring, 105.
          Method of despatch to market, 110.   Effect of former
          prohibition of trawling, 103.   Dimensions of nets and
          boats, 105. Physique and character of the trawl fisher-

men, 115. Number of men employed, 106. Long prosecuted on Lochfyne, 111 Pennant on fishing, 112.

Horses, cost of, in Bruce's time, 24.

Isthmus of Tarbert described as a " sandy ridge," 5 ; origin of name, 4 ; frequent transport of boats across it, 30 ; crossed by Magnus Barefoot, Haco, and Bruce (see under these heads) ; formerly guarded by three castles, 16 ; extent, 2.

Islay. Bailie of Islay contributes to castle, 25 ; horses and provisions got from Islay (1326), 24.

Isles, Angus Og of the, 11 ; John of the Isles, 27 ; Reginald of the Isles, 7.

Isle, house in the, 22.

Isles, sheriffdom of the South, 47.

James IV. repairs castle and provides it with artillery, 33 ; holds Parliament at Tarbert (1494), 33 ; visits Tarbert (1498), 34 ; resides in castle (1499), 35 ; grants keeping of Tarbert Castle to Argyll (1499), 36.

James VI. proposes to visit Tarbert (1600), 52.

John of the Isles, negotiations with, 27.

Jones, Paul, and the Tarbert packet, 141.

Kilberry. See Campbell.

Kilcalmonell church and church-lands, 9 ; Tarbert situated partly in Kilcalmonell parish, 94.

Kildusclan, 79.

Kiln, lime (1326),17.

Kintarbert. See Campbell.

Kintyre one of the south isles, 3 ; legend of Bruce and Douglas, 129 ; granted to Argyll, 54 ; ravaged by Haco, 7 ; ravaged by Alister M'Donald, 58 ; Tarbert village situated partly in Kintyre, 94 ; Bailie of Kintyre contributes to Tarbert Castle, 25.

Kitchen at castle (1326), 17 ; John, clerk of the kitchen, 22.

Knapdale, ownership of lands of, 37 ; Tarbert village, situated partly in South Knapdale, 94.

Lamberton, Bishop, resides in Tarbert Castle (1326), 18.

Lands, ownership of, 37.

Largie and the '45, 70.

Lawsuit as to Tarbert feu charter, 79.

Leslie, General, at Tarbert isthmus, 58.

Levies in Tarbertshire, 49.

Lime, cost of burning, 23 ; lime kiln, 17.

Magnus Barefoot " sails across isthmus of Tarbert," 3.

Malt house, 21.

Marts, cost of keeping, 22.

Meal, largely used in Bruce's reign, 24 ; Cost, 24.

Military preparations (1684), 61.

Mill with pond and lade, 21.

Moat of Castle, 21.

Moles, late coming into Kintyre, connected with the Campbells, 126.

Money, value of, 20.

Moray, John, Earl of, resides in castle, 27.

Muckroy, 79.

M'Alisters of Tarbert, 72 ; their descent, 72 ; Donald, 73 ; Charles, 73 ; Archibald (apparent), 73 ; Ronald, 73 ; Archibald, 73 ; Charles, 73 ; Archibald, 74 ; extent of M'Alister's lands, 78 ; raid in 1602, 75 ; forays in 1685, 75 ; conflict with the M'Ivers, 74.

M'Ay, Gilchrist, contributes to the building of Tarbert Castle, 25.

M'Donald, Coll, see Coll Ciotach.

M'Donald, John, Bailie of Islay, contributes to building of castle, 25.

M'Donald of Largie and the '45, 70.

M'Donald, Sir Alister, ravages Kintyre, 58.

M'Donald, Sir James, raises his clansmen against the Campbells (1615), 54.

M'Gilchrist, Donald, Lord of Tarbard, grants a charter to monks of Paisley, 9.

M'Gilhon, Dofnald, Neil, and John, give assistance at building of Tarbert Castle, 25.

M'Ivers defeated by M'Allister of Tarbert, 74.

M'Lean, Alan, see Ailean-nan-Sop.

M'Lean of Coll. See Coll.

M'Lean, Sir Lachlan, represents Tarbert in Parliament (1633), 46.

Nets. See herring fishery.

Newbattle, Abbot of, contributes to "the bigin of Tarbert,"
34.

Origin of name, "Tarbert," 4.
Orthography of Tarbert, 4.

Paisley. Charter by MacGilchrist to monks of Paisley, 9 ;
possessions of the monks of Paisley in Kilcalmonell,
10 ; Abbot of Paisley contributes to the building of
Tarbert Castle, 25.
Park of Tarbert, 25.
Parliament at Tarbert, 33.
Parochial arrangements, 94.
Passage, submarine, from castle, 124.
Pele at West Tarbert, 23.
Piers and quays, 91, 94, 141.
Plumber's Wages, 23.
Poultry, cost of keeping, 22.

Quay. See Pier.
Queen's sheep, cost of watching the, 22.

Raids, 75.
Reginald, King of the Isles, 7.
Road between the two Tarberts, 23 ; Sliabh Ghaoil road, 84.
Robert I. See Bruce.
Robert II. said to have been keeper of Tarbert Castle, 26.
Roofing, cost of (1326), 23.
Roundheads in possession of castle, 59 ; garrison surprised
by the Highlanders (1652), 59.

School, 96.
Scott's "Lord of the Isles," extract from, 15.
Shairp's "Kilmahoe," extract from, 5.
Sheriff of South Isles to have his seat at Tarbert or Loch-
kilkerran, 47.
Ship, the king's great, at Tarbert, 26.
Shire of Tarbert. Established previously to 1841, 45 ; united
to Argyllshire (1633), 46 ; Earl of Argyll sheriff of
Tarbert, 46 ; levies in Tarbetshire, 49 ; taxation of
Tarbert, 50 ; extent of the shire, 46. Name of Tar-
bertshire still used after its union to Argyll, 47.

INDEX—*continued.*

Skipness. Entries referring to it in Constable of Tarbert's
    account, 22. Conditions upon which it was held from
    Argyll, 80. Anna Campbell, daughter of Walter
    Campbell, of Skipness, 74.
Sliabh Ghaoil Road, 84. Legend of Bruce on Sliabh
    Ghaoil, 129.
Snorro's description of the isthmus, 4.
Sodor, Bishop of, contributes to building of castle, 25.
Steward, Earl of Menthet or Menteith, 37. Walter, high
    steward of Scotland, at Tarbert (1315), 14.
Stonefield. See Campbell.
Syfyn or Sween of Argyll, 10, 37.
Swine (1326), 22.

Taxation of Tarbert burgh, 29. Taxation of Tarbertshire, 50.
Templars (I.O.G.T.) 97 ; hall, 98.
Tides in East and West Loch Tarbert, 140.
Towers of Castle, 123.
Trawling. See Herring Fishery.

Volunteers, 98.

Walks around Tarbert, 130.
Wapenschaws, 48.
Wax for the chapel, 22.
West Loch Tarbert. Extent, 138. Scenery, 134. Tides, 140.
    Macculloch's description of, 139. Rambles in the
    neighbourhood, 134.
West Tarbert village, 136. Distillery, 136. Pele, 23.
    Quay, 141.
Wine house, 21. Wine bought by Bruce at Tarbert, 26.

TARBERT PAST AND PRESENT.

CHAPTER I.

EARLY GLIMPSES.

TO many minds of an antiquarian or archæo-logical tendency, minds that love to wander 'mong the things of a bygone age, the associations which cluster themselves around the old historic village, or cling tenaciously as its trailing ivy to the picturesque though dilapidated ruin which has braved the storms of centuries—which has seen thrones established and dynasties overturned, con-stitute a theme of interest and attraction.   To such an one every step taken among these relics of the past serves anew to fire his imagination; every chamber, nook, or dungeon of the now deserted castle tells again its wondrous tale, its varied tale of love and war; and, standing on its crumbling walls, he finds himself conjuring up the approach of the enemy, or planning a sortie for its relief.

The strategical importance of Tarbert with its castle, commanding as it does the shortest and safest route from the Western Islands to the firth of Clyde, the prominent historical events in which it has figured, and other circumstances such as the details of the building of the castle, that shall appear later, serve to link it in a not unimportant manner with the memories of the past, and to call up, not only the jealous rivalries of clans with their incessant quarrels, but to lead us back to the time when Scotland's history proper was yet in its early infancy.

Beautifully situated around the margin of its land-locked bay, it rejoices in a name, in one or other of its forms, as *Tarbert, Tarbet* or *Tarbat,* possibly the commonest in Scotland. Amongst the most familiar are Tarbet on Lochlomond, Tarbet East and West in Jura, and Tarbert East and West in Harris; and, in common with all of them, Tarbert on Lochfyne owes its name, it would appear, to circumstances dependent on its geographical position. Stretching from the eastern loch to the western, and presenting an effectual barrier to their union, is a narrow neck of land, fully three-quarters of a mile in breadth, joining Kintyre to the mainland, and known as the Isthmus of Tarbert. That these lochs should be united and their waters mingled has doubtless been the desire of centuries, and the present canal scheme, as well as its more immediate predecessors, is but the echo of bygone dreams.

The manner in which the obstacle to navigation presented by the isthmus has been hitherto practically overcome upon a small scale, seems to account for the origin of the name. It is not, however, as a matter of convenience or necessity, but as one of cunning and aggrandizement that history first informs us of the method of accomplishment.

It was the year 1098. Looming out of the darkness which enshrouds this period of Scottish history, we catch a romantic glimpse of it through the medium of Scandinavian records. Torfæns, in his Hist. Orcad., informs us that Magnus Barefoot, King of Norway, having shortly before conquered the Hebrides, concluded a treaty with the Scottish King. This treaty was to the effect that all the Western Isles, or all those places that could be circumnavigated, should be ceded to the Norwegian King. Not satisfied, however, with the ordinary interpretation of the treaty, Magnus contrived to add to his possessions the rich peninsula of Kintyre by a species of ingenious fraud. Seizing the helm as he seated himself in the stern of his lightest galley, he had himself drawn across the narrow isthmus in a sort of triumphal progress, by which means it was conceded in these simple times he had demonstrated Kintyre to be an island. At any rate, as the result probably of this exploit, the peninsula was reckoned one of the South Isles, or Sudreys, until the seventeenth century, and it is generally believed that from this custom of transporting boats from the one loch to the other Tarbert has derived its name, it being supposed to be compounded of the two Gaelic words, *tarruing*, to draw, and *bata*, a boat ; while the fact of this royal stratagem having occurred here may account, as Pennant imagines, for Tarbert on Lochfyne being designated in all old writings as *the* Tarbert.

The system of drawing boats across isthmuses to avoid long or dangerous navigations was not at all uncommon among the ancients. Among the Greeks such positions received a name meaning dragging places, and a very remarkable one existed near Corinth.

The varied forms under which the name Tarbert appears at different periods are interesting as showing at least the ingenuity of the writers. It would be somewhat of a test of ingenuity to add to the variety. In the oldest records we find it spelt as Tarbart. Soon it takes the form of Tarbard, and later it appears indiscriminately as Terbert, Tarbert, Tarbett, Tarbet, Tarbatt, Tarbat, Torban, Tarbot, Tarbitt, Terbat, Turbet, and Terbart.

That the old sea king was thoroughly acquainted with the value of Kintyre as a possession is rendered probable by a remark which occurs in a Scandinavian record of the thirteenth century, the "Magnus Saga" of Snorro, in which, after describ-

ing Magnus' boat stratagem, he says:—" Satiri
(Kintyre) is a great country, and better than any
island of the Sudreys, Man excepted." And then,
describing the isthmus, he ʔdds—" There is a
narrow sandy ridge between it and Scotland, so
that ships are often drawn across it."

The following passage from the late Principal
Shairp's poem of " Kilmahoe " refers to the above
incident:—

> " Then Norroway kings, our chiefs o'erthrown,
>   Held isle and islet for their own,
>   And one, more haughty than the rest,
>   Swore he would claim for island ground
>   Whate'er he drove his galley round ;
>   And from the Atlantic, up the west,
>   Loch Tarbert bearing, made them haul
>   His barge across that isthmus small ;
>   Himself proud seated at the helm.
>   Then spreading sail down fair Lochfyne,
>   He cried aloud, ' Kintyre is mine,
>   I've bound it to my island realm.' "

To Highlanders the explanation given by Snorro
regarding the surname received by Magnus is not a
little interesting. It is to the effect that the
Scandinavian monarch so admired the " Garb of
Old Gaul," that on his return to Norway he himself adopted it, and hence received the appellation
of Barefoot.

Regarding Tarbert, history now becomes silent
for many years, and for the next incident connected
with it we are again indebted to Norse records.

It is very similar to that which has just been
described, and is quoted by Carlyle, in " The Early
Kings of Norway."

After referring to the authenticity of the battle
of Largs in 1263, and to Haco's evident " high
kind of humour" previous to it, he goes on to
quote from the records as follows:—" While his
ships and army were doubling the Mull of Cantyre,
he had his own boat set on wheels, and therein,
splendidly enough, had himself drawn across the
promontory at a flatter part. 'All to the left of
me is mine and Norway's!' exclaimed Hakon in
his triumphal boat progress, which such disasters
soon followed."

The disasters referred to were those resulting
from the battle of Largs, which was fought shortly
afterwards. The storms of an unusually severe
winter fought on the side of the Scots, and enabled
them to effect the utter ruin of the Norwegian
expedition—an expedition which, as represented
by their own historians, was the most formidable
that ever left the ports of Norway. It consisted
of from one hundred to one hundred and forty
ships, carying twenty thousand men. On his way
home Haco died at the Orkneys, it is said of a
broken heart. His son Magnus readily concluded
a treaty with the Scottish King, Alexander III.,
in which all Norse claims to Kintyre and the
Western Isles were for ever renounced.

In those days, and particularly on occasions such as those referred to, the position occupied by the Kings of the Isles was peculiarly delicate. By no means a match for the neighbouring states of Scotland and Scandinavia, they were usually under allegiance to one or other of them. Though this homage was of course involuntary, when they were in straits they considered it implied protection; and when that was not afforded, they had little hesitation in forming new connections more conducive to their safety.

On the occasion of the battle of Largs, all the powerful chiefs of the Isles and Western Highlands, with the exception of Eogan (John) of Argyll (who held faithfully by the Scottish King, and strove to bring about a cessation of hostilities), fought on the side of the Norwegians, and that apparently with great bravery. In Haco's own ship, according to the Norse records from which what follows is taken, we find Roderick, the second son of King Reginald of the Isles, occupying an important position, and when the expedition had reached the island of Kerrera, opposite Oban, it was joined by Roderick's three sons, King Dugald, Allan, and Angus. Regarding the Lords of Kintyre and Islay, they were apparently under allegiance to Alexander, and it required some compulsion to make them join the forces of Haco. From Kerrera the latter sent fifty ships south to the Mull of Kintyre to plunder, under the command of King Dugald and other prominent captains, where "they burnt hamlets and took all the effects that they could find. They killed some of the inhabitants; the rest fled where they could." On the promise that the peninsula should be spared from further devastation, Margad or Murchard (Murdoch), Lord of Kintyre, surrendered his lands to Haco, as likewise did Angus, the Lord of Islay, both taking the oath of allegiance and delivering hostages. Notwithstanding this, Haco laid on their estates a fine of a thousand head of cattle, but "returned Islay to Angus upon the same terms that the other barons in the Hebrides enjoyed their lands."

After the battle we learn that King Dugald and Allan, his brother, took leave of the Norwegians at Tobermory, having previously received, as rewards, grants of those lands formerly owned by Eogan of Argyll, under Haco's sovereignty. On Dugald, also, was bestowed a castle in South Kintyre (probably Dunaverty) which had been besieged and taken the previous summer. To Murchard of Kintyre was given the Island of Arran, and to Roderick the Island of Bute. They were among the last gifts of a king who had already reigned the long period of forty-six years, and who was soon to pass away from the scenes of his many strifes.

During this century, and about the period we have been referring to, the lands of Tarbert seem to have been in the possession of the M'Gilchrists. The ecclesiastical matters of the district at this

time were under the jurisdiction of the Monks of
Paisley, and from the register of that Monastery we
may trace the connection as far back as the middle
of this century. About the year 1250 "Donenald
Makgilcriste, Lord of Tarbard," granted to the
Monks of Paisley a charter conferring upon them
the right to cut timber on his lands.

Though this charter contains no internal evidence
that the "Tarbard" referred to is that with which
we are concerned, various considerations have led
many to believe that such is the case. As a specimen
of a charter of these early days, as well as for its
inherent interest, it is worth quoting in full. Like
all learned documents of these days, the original is
in Latin :—

"CHARTER OF DONALD MAKGILCRISTE, LORD OF TARBARD.

To all the sons of holy mother church now and to be (or
present and future) Donenald Makgilcriste, Lord of Tarbard,
sends eternal greeting in the Lord. Know that I with a
devout mind have granted, and by this my present charter,
for the salvation of the souls of my ancestors and for the
salvation of my own soul, have given in pure and perpetual
alms on behalf of me and my heirs to God, St. James and
St. Mirin of Paisley, and the monks there serving God and
to serve him for ever, the free right of cutting, taking, and
carrying away all kinds of timber pleasing to those "religious," for the building and maintaining of their monastery
and house of Paisley, within all the woods of my whole land.
I give also and grant on behalf of me and my heirs to the
same "religious " and their men for ever as free entry and
exit with all kinds of timber cut, or about to be cut and
carried away as the free right of cutting, taking and carrying

away without the oversight of the sergeant. In testimony of which thing I have affixed my seal to my present charter. These being witnesses, Sir Hugh of Parlciner, perpetual vicar of Kylmacolme ; Sir Nicholas, chaplain ; Sir Malcolm, chaplain."

Ten years later the connection of the monks of Paisley with the Parish of Kilcalmonell was drawn still closer. From the "Origines Parochiales Scotiæ," we learn that in 1261 the lay patron, "Dufgall the son of Syfyn (or Sween) granted to the monks of Paisley, with the consent of John, his heir, the right of patronage of the church of St. Calmanel, which was situated in his land of Kentyr, with the chapel of St. Columba, which was situated near his castle of Schepehinche (Skipness) after the death of Clement, rector of the said church, bequeathing his body at same time to be buried in the monastery of Paisley."

For centuries the church of Kilcalmonell, situated first at Balinakill and later at Clachan (both about eleven miles from Tarbert), as well as the lands connected with it, continued as part of the barony or lordship of Paisley.

CHAPTER II.

TARBERT IN THE FOURTEENTH CENTURY.

ELIEVED in the manner above detailed from the frequent harassments of the Northern Power, Scotland soon found herself called upon to engage her whole energies in repelling the presumption of her southern neighbour. It is in connection with this long-sustained struggle for independence that Tarbert next appears (this time in traditional story), and again a royal visitor is the occasion. That visitor is Robert the Bruce, and the year 1306. Not, however, in the pomp and pride of power, surrounded by thousands of followers does he appear, but as a downcast fugitive king, passing, by this route, it is said, after his defeat at Methven, with a mere handful of staunch adherents to seek a refuge in Kintyre with Angus Og, commonly called Lord of the Isles. This refuge and protection Angus readily accorded him, first at

Saddell and afterwards at Dunaverty, and later on, when circumstances required it, conveyed him for greater security to the island of Rathlin, on the Irish coast.

Cuthbert Bede in his "Glencreggan" gives the following legend in connection with the King's wanderings on this occasion. (The mountain referred to is within a few miles of Tarbert) :—
" On the bleak mountain in South Knapdale, called Sliabh-Ghaoil, the hunted monarch passed a cheerless night. He was well-nigh spent with fatigue and hunger, and, to add to his distress, the night was bitterly cold. He would probably have perished had not a goat come to him and laid herself down beside him. She suffered him to refresh himself with her milk, and kept him warm all the night through. Refreshed by the night's rest, and the goat's milk and warmth, the Bruce came on to Cantire the next morning. It was in grateful memory of this that, when he 'enjoyed his own agen,' he made a law that forbade any one to poind (or pound) a goat."

A period of eight years of varied fortune, eight years mainly of hardship and defeat, has slowly passed, and at last the Bruce's star shoots brilliantly above the horizon. Bannockburn is fought, and Scotland is forever free.

The task which the king found before him of introducing order into his long troubled dominions was one of no light nature, and this, it will be

understood, was more particularly true of the Highlands and Western Isles. After his brother Edward
had departed on his ill-starred expedition to Ireland,
King Robert set out on a visit to the Isles, and on
his way thither chose the route across the isthmus
of Tarbert. According to Barbour, Archdeacon of
Aberdeen, who wrote his poem "The Bruce" in
1375, the following is the manner in which the land
part of the journey was accomplished. The distance
between the two lochs was "lompnyt all with treis,"
which phrase may either mean that a smooth slide
of planks was constructed, or that the trunks of
trees were so arranged as to form rollers. Taking
advantage of a favourable wind that was blowing,
the galleys were placed on the structure, all the
sails were set in order to assist their progress, the
men were set to work, and so, by means of this
unique combination of sailing and hauling on dry
land, the western loch was reached. There is a
tradition that in the journey one of the ships fell
and was seriously damaged, and the place where
the accident occurred is still pointed out.

It is not improbable that the overland route was
selected by Bruce in order to work on the super-
stitious feelings of the Islesmen, amongst whom,
according to Barbour, an old prophecy was current,
possibly dating from the time of Magnus Barefoot's
successful stratagem, to the effect that, if their
invader should sail across this isthmus, all resistance to his might would be unavailing. So effective

was the king's device in attaining the desired end
that all the rebels, with the exception of the Lord
of Lorne, submitted without any show of resistance.

The following, which are Barbour's lines describing the above incident, are worth quoting for their
interest and quaintness :—

" Quhen he (King Robert) had conwoyit to the se
    His brodyr Eduuard, and his menye,
    With his shippis he made him yare
    Into the Ilis for to fayr.
    Walter Stewart with him tuk he,
    His maich, and with him gret menye,
    And other men of gret noblay.
    To Tarbart they held thair way,
    In galayis ordanyt for thair far,
    Bot thaim worthyt draw thair schippis thar :
    And a myle wes betuix the seys ;
    Bot that wes lompnyt all with treis.
    The king his schippis thar gert draw.
    And for the wynd couth stoutly blaw
    Apon thair bak, as thai wald ga,
    He gert men rapis and mastis ta,
    And set thaim in the schippis hey,
    And sayllis to the toppis tey ;
    And gert men gang thar by drawand.
    The wynd thaim helpyt that wes blawand ;
    Swa that, in a litill space,
    Thair flote all our drawin was,

    And quhen thai that in the Ilis war,
    Hard tell how the gud king had thar
    Gert his schippis with saillis ga
    Owt our betuix the Tarbartis twa,
    Thai war abaysit sa wtrely.
    For thai wyst, throw auld prophecy,
    That he that suld ger schippis sua

Betuix thai seis with saillis ga,
Suld wyne the Ilis sua till haud,
That nane with strenth suld him withstand.
Tharfor thai come all to the king.
Wes nane withstud his bidding,
Owtakny Jhone of Lorne allayne,
Bot weill sone eftre wes he tayne."

Sir Walter Scott, in his "Lord of the Isles," makes use of the above incident, and, applying it to an earlier date, describes an imaginary journey of the Bruce across the isthmus, when on his way from Rathlin to Ayrshire in 1307.

" Ever the breeze blows merrily,
  But the galley ploughs no more the sea.
  Lest rounding wild Cantire they meet
  The southern foeman's watchful fleet,
    They held unwonted way ;—
  Up Tarbat's western lake they bore,
  They dragg'd their bark the isthmus o'er,
  As far as Kilmaconnel's shore,
    Upon the eastern bay.
  It was a wondrous sight to see
  Topmast and pennon glitter free,
  High raised above the greenwood tree,
  As on dry land the galley moves,
  By cliff and copse and alder groves.
  Deep import from that selcouth sign
  Did many a mountain seer divine,
  For ancient legends told the Gael
  That when a royal bark should sail
    O'er Kilmaconnel moss,
  Old Albyn should in fight prevail,
  And every foe should faint and quail
    Before her silver Cross."

In the year 1325 Bruce commenced the building of Tarbert Castle. The knowledge gained by him during former visits of the strategical importance of the isthmus, the dread with which the navigation of the Mull of Kintyre was at that time regarded, and the consequent frequency of transporting the small ships of war then in use across this narrow neck, together with the necessity he felt of having a convenient base of operations from which to keep the Islemen in check, constituted sufficient stimulus for its erection.

In addition to Tarbert Castle, we are informed that other two forts guarded the isthmus, one about its middle, in the neighbourhood of Cairnbaan, and the other at the head of the West Loch. These, however, must have been of small size, and all trace of them has long since disappeared.

Whether or not there existed, previous to the time of Bruce, any fort on the same site as the present castle was erected, is a question that cannot easily be determined. Cosmo Innes, Burnet, and Taylor assert that the castle was first built by King Robert, while Gregory, in his "History of the Highlands and the Western Isles," holds to the opinion that fortifications did previously exist, and that Bruce's efforts were directed to the strengthening and extending of them, and to the furnishing of them with a Royal garrison. Tytler, again, more than once makes a similar statement, and asserts that there existed a Royal castle as early as the reign of Edward I. of England. The fact, also, that the Exchequer Roll, which details the expenses connected with Bruce's castle, also mentions the repairing of houses, "placing a *new* vat in the brew-house, making a *new* kitchen, lime-kiln," &c., points in the direction of former ones having existed. The expenses, however, connected with these matters are but a very small fraction of the amount incurred at this time in connection with the general structure.

The probability is that a fort did formerly exist, that it was built by the Lords of the Isles, and its keeping committed to the M'Gilchrists as Lords of Tarbert; and that later when Alexander, Lord of the Isles, resigned his lands, &c., in 1315, it fell to the Crown. It is reasonable, at any rate, to suppose that a position that was really the key to Kintyre (the cradle of the Scottish Monarchy) would not be left entirely unprotected.

Standing proudly against the sky upon its commanding height, and bearing well its centuries of age, Tarbert Castle still exists as a stately and picturesque ruin. Situated on the south side of the loch about one hundred feet above sea level, few castles can be said to command so extensive and so varied a view, a fact which must have added very considerably to its efficiency. Glancing the eye to the south and east, it scans the coast of Bute, and ranges along the Cowal shore from Ardlamont point to Otter spit. Northward, Ben

Cruachan, Loch Awe's proud guardian, and the upper reaches of the blue Lochfyne, come well into view; while to the westward West Loch Tarbert, with its surrounding hills clad in their mantle of green, are seen stretching away in soft and mazy beauty.

Originally the castle would appear to have consisted of a strong, high, square tower, with extensive subsidiary buildings, and numerous round towers, constructed of durable whinstone and red sandstone. Approachable only from one direction, and guarded by a moat and widely extended walls, it must have been at the time of its power quite impregnable to any engines of war that could then be brought against it.

The year in which the building of the castle was commenced saw Bruce land once more on the isthmus of Tarbert. From this fact we may infer that his thorough knowledge of military affairs, and the necessities of the situation, was brought to bear, if not in selecting the site (than which a better could not have been chosen) at any rate in determining the form the structure should take. Some of the contracts, indeed, would appear to have been entered into during this visit.

That the king took very considerable interest in its erection is evidenced by the fact that he again visited Tarbert the following year, and resided in the castle for some time. On this occasion he was accompanied by his warm friends, Lamberton,

Bishop of St. Andrews, and Primate of Scotland, and the Good Lord Douglas, names well-known and loved by all Scottish readers of the annals of the wars of independence. Very probably, also, he had in his train the Lords Auditors of the Exchequer, for we learn that during this visit "he received the accounts of several of the local stewards." In these days the officers who collected the king's revenues, of every grade from sheriffs to bailies and custumars, rendered their accounts yearly before the Lords Auditors, receiving due notice to attend at a given time and place. On such occasions the Lords usually sat from four to six weeks, changing their place of sitting if the king shifted his residence during that period.

The interest attaching to the building of Tarbert Castle is much enhanced by the important circumstance that the details regarding it, and furnished in the year of the latter visit (1326) by the then Constable of Tarbert, John De Lany, constitute, according to the editors of the " Origines Parochiales Scotiæ," " the earliest account of any details of domestic architecture and modes of rural life in Scotland."

Indeed, the earliest Scottish Exchequer Roll extant is that contributed by the Constable of Tarbert, the earlier ones having been destroyed or lost during the wars referred to above. In the original Latin this interesting document may be found in the " Exchequer Rolls of Scotland," and

the "Compota Cameraria Scotiæ," while an English
translation of the greater portion is given in the
" Origines Parochiales Scotiæ."

Though the castle, as at first designed, appears
never to have been quite completed, it would seem
that at the date when the accounts were rendered
by the Constable, viz., 20th July, 1326, almost all
that was then purposed being done was finished.
We have therefore in this Roll what must be considered a tolerably complete statement of the outlay
connected with the building itself, as well as of
some other matters more or less intimately connected with it, and an examination and comparison
of the extent of building that could be constructed
out of a few hundreds of pounds in the fourteenth
century with what can be effected in the last
quarter of the nineteenth century with the same
amount, would be not a little interesting and
instructive.

From this record we learn that from the 18th
day of April, 1325, to the 20th July of the following
year, the whole amount received by the Constable
for the building of the castle and other duties connected with his office was £518 13s 8d. During
the same period he had expended, in all, £511.

In passing, it may be noted that at this date the
current money of Scotland did not materially differ
in value from that of the sister country, Scots
money passing for its full value in England in the
reign of Robert the Bruce, and down till about the

year 1355. The depreciation of the currency in Scotland which ultimately brought the pound Scots down to one twelfth of the pound sterling, belongs to a later age. During Bruce's reign the pound weight of silver was coined into twenty-six shillings and threepence; at the present day the same weight is made into sixty-six shillings.

Apart from the dimensions of the castle, which cannot be gathered from any of the records, a good idea of its extent may be inferred from a mere enumeration of the various accessory structures with which it was provided, so far as referred to in connection with payments. Separate from the main building, which must have contained accommodation for a considerable body of men, mention is made of a hall built on piers, houses within the inner court with a middle wall enclosing it, and a chapel, together with such subsidiary structures as a wine house, bakehouse, goldsmith's house, a malthouse, brew-house, and a mill with its mill-pond and lade, and lastly, a moat.

For the expenses connected with some of these buildings, viz., the houses within the inner court, the middle wall enclosing it, and the wine house, the Constable had not leisure to account, and they are therefore not included in the £511 expended at the date mentioned. Among others, however, the following items, which have no direct connection with the building itself, are included in the statement of expenditure, and when these are also taken

into account, the value of money at this particular
period will be more fully realised. Some of the
entries are further rather peculiar, and serve to
throw a little light on the habits and modes of life
of that far away time.

In connection with the king's visit, it is noted
that James Del More received the sum of £2 1s
"to make provision at Tarbert for the king's need,"
while at the same time there was delivered to
"John, clerk of the kitchen," twelve codri of cheese
valued at 12s. In preparation for the other guests,
a sum of 2s 2½d was expended in providing "litter
for the chambers of the Lord Bishop of St. Andrews
and Sir James, Lord of Douglas, with the cutting
and carriage of branches of birch for repairing the
hall and chambers." For "keeping forty of the
queen's sheep before the arrival of the king," 1s;
"keeping the poultry for fifteen days," 1s 10½d;
"keeping the king's marts and swine by two
shepherds and two lads," seven bolls of meal;
"watching bran for the dogs at Wester Tarbart for
three weeks," 2s 6d; to "Copin Wef, the merchant,
by the king's order, for cloths bought of him at
Tarbert," £1 6s 8d; "carriage of bread from Tarbert
to Skipness," 1s 10d; "driving marts to Skipness
twice," 8d. Besides these there were also included
the Constable's salary, Sir Maurice the Chaplain's
salary, wax for the chapel, "building a house in the
isle anew, with roofing for the same;" "one hundred
large boards bought and sent to Cardross for repair-

ing the park," 3s 4d; "keeping and watching a prisoner," 3s 4d; "part payment for building a new pele (fort) at Wester Tarbert," £4; to William Scott, £8 "as part payment of £13 6s 8d, agreed for with him for making a road from the one Tarbert to the other," &c., &c.

As was to have been expected, more particularly in connection with such a building as the castle, the great bulk of the expenditure was on mason work. To Robert, the principal contractor for the mason work, a sum of £282 15s was paid, besides a gratuity of £5 6s 8d, "because in the king's absence he had built the walls wider than agreed on." John, another mason, received £28 7s 8d "by bargain for building the said castle;" while Adam, a third mason, was paid "by covenant for building the said castle, £9 10s;" and a further sum of £50 "for burning seven hundred and sixty chalders of lime for that building." The roofing of the "houses in the castle" is stated as having occupied two roofers for forty days, and for this large undertaking they were rewarded with the sum of 13s 4d, just twopence a day for each man.

Of the skilled workmen whose wages are specified the best paid was the smith, who received ninepence per day. Next to him came the plumber, with eightpence a day; while the carpenter got sixpence a day. Compared with these the stipend of Sir Maurice the Chaplain cannot be considered very satisfactory, for it is put down at the modest

sum of £2 for the half year.   Indeed, when we find
that even the Constable, the chief officer of the
castle, was content to receive a shilling a day, it is
evident that the skilled workman who received
his eightpence or ninepence was a most important
individual, and most probably very well off with
his seemingly modest wage.

But if wages were small, the price of provisions
was of course correspondingly low.   The materials
entering most largely into the dietary of the period
were oatmeal and cheese.   From numerous entries
in the accounts, it is evident that the chief source
from which these commodities were obtained was
Islay, and they were supplied in such quantities
that large consignments were made to the king at
Cardross, and to the chamberlain, "Sir Robert of
Peblis."   When provisions formed part of the wages
of a workman, these were the articles supplied, and
the allowance given to a man for a month was
generally one boll of meal and one codrus (about a
stone) of cheese, the whole being valued at two
shillings and sixpence.   Other things were also
equally low in price.   Sixteen chalders of coal,
equal to twenty-four tons, cost only twenty-one
shillings and fourpence, and was used for "the
work done by Patrick the smith."   Mention is
further made of five horses "for the carriage of
lime," having been purchased for £1 17s.   The
expenses connected with bringing four of them from
Islay was but ten shillings and sixpence, including

sixpence which the man who had gone for them was pleased to receive as wages.

From these same records out of which the above particulars have been gleaned, a full statement may be gathered of the sources from which the funds for the buildings, &c., were obtained. By far the greater part was provided by the gentlemen in authority all round the west coast. Dugald Campbell, Sheriff of Argyll (or Ergadia, as it was then written), and Bailie of Athole, is credited with contributing a considerable portion, while a larger amount in the shape of oatmeal and cheese was forwarded by John M'Donald, bailie of Islay. Assistance was also rendered by "Dofnald, Neil and John M'Gilhon"—the last of them the ancestor of the M'Lean's of Duart. Contributions are further acknowledged from "Gilchrist M'Ay" (the progenitor of the M'Kays of Ugadale), from the Bishop of Sodor, the Rector of Arran, the Abbot of Paisley, the Bailie of Kintyre, &c.

In the records of the year 1329 acknowledgment is made of £7 having been received by De Lany "out of the farms of Buchan, for the work of Tarbert," and of a sum of £2 from a William of Bonkill. Notices in connection with expenditure at this time include an entry in this same year of £2 as part payment to William Scott for "making and maintaining the park of Tarbert," and a further sum of £5 to the same individual in 1330 as allowance in full for the said park.

On completion of the castle sufficiently to fit it for its intended service, a keeper would be doubtless appointed by the Bruce. Recognizing its position as the most important on the Argyll coast, the first on whom he bestowed the office is said (but on doubtful authority) to have been his grandson, Robert Steward, who afterwards became Robert II. of Scotland.

Whether or not after the year 1326 the King again visited Tarbert we have no certain information. Residing as he did so frequently at Cardross, a very few hours with a favourable breeze would suffice to carry him through the Kyles of Bute, and across the waters of Lochfyne. Two entries, in which it is stated that wine and salt were bought " by the king at Tarbert" in 1329, may warrant the inference that he was resident in the castle in this year. Two other items in the accounts of the same year may point also in this direction. They refer to the " king's great ship." The first is one of eighteen shillings paid to twelve men passing from Dumbarton to Tarbert, " to bring back the great ship belonging to the king," while the other takes note of six shillings paid to nine men " passing with John, the son of Gun, to Tarbert, with the rigging of the king's great ship." The inference is further strengthened by the fact of a Court Jester having been brought to Tarbert in 1329, the entry referring to it stating that eighteenpence was paid for " the expenses of the men who accompanied Patrick, the fool, from England to Tarbert."

The first occurrence of imperial interest in which, as far as is known, the central position of the castle was utilized took place in the year 1335.

Ere this date the Bruce had gone " the way of all the earth," as also had Angus, the Lord of the Isles, his staunch ally at Bannockburn. John, the successor of the latter, failed to follow the example of his father in his warm adherence to the Scottish Monarchy, but as Fordun, the historian, mildly puts it " favoured the English interest."

This position of affairs being highly unsatisfactory and prejudicial to the well-being of Scotland, it was considered extremely desirable to endeavour to come to some arrangement, and in order the more expeditiously and conveniently to carry out negotiations with this descendant of the " mighty Somerled," John, Earl of Moray, the guardian of Scotland, resided within the castle of Tarbert for a considerable portion of the time during which the negotiations were proceeding. Before they were completed he was called south to repel an invasion of French troops who had come to assist the English.

The visitor to Tarbert never fails to note the particularly secure natural harbour with which it is endowed, and around which its houses are grouped. This fact of a commodious and safe anchorage, together with its proximity to West

Loch Tarbert, and its comparative nearness to the important ports on the Firth of Clyde have constituted it, from the earliest period in which the necessity for such existed, the centre of export for the surrounding district, as well as for Islay and others of the southern isles.

Evidence is found in connection with the customs of its occupying this position as early at any rate as 1328.

During the time of Robert the Bruce the "great custom" was charged on three classes of exports, viz., wool, wool-fels (sheep skins with the wool on), and hides. In the year above referred to a charge of seven shillings and eight pence is made by "Sir Robert of Peblis," Chamberlain of Scotland, for "making a coket for the burgh of Tarbert," the use of which and its necessity will be understood by a reference to the following extract from the preface to vol. I. of the Exchequer Rolls already mentioned.

"Merchandize liable to custom could not be legally exported without a cocket, that is a certificate under the seal of the proper officer, that the great custom had been paid on it; and every burgh of export had its cocket seal and cocket clerk. One of the items of expenditure in the Chamberlain's account of 1328 is the making of a coket (that is a cocket seal) for the burgh of Tarbert. . . .
When goods were shipped at one port under the coket of another, they were included in the articles charged for, but the cocket appeared on the credit

side of the account; and we find the custumars of Berwick, Edinburgh, Aberdeen, and Perth, crediting themselves on various occasions with cockets not only of the royal burghs of Linlithgow, Inverkeithing, Stirling, Cupar, and Tarbert, but of the Earl of Moray's burgh of Lochmaben, and of the church burgh of Dunfermline.   .   .   .   .

The custumars were persons appointed by the Crown in each burgh of export, being generally one or two of the leading burgesses to collect the king's great custom."

In this extract, it will be observed, Tarbert is classed as one of the royal burghs, and in the accounts of this period it is frequently referred to as "the burgh of Tarbard." Regarding the date of its erection as such, it is improbable it occurred before the reign of Robert Bruce. According to Bell's "Law of Scotland," royal burghs, as a rule, sprung up beside royal castles, and this is stated in the preface just quoted from to have been apparently the case with regard to Tarbert.

One of the privileges of royal burghs at this time was that they were required to contribute to the support of the country in the shape of taxes, and in the year 1329 Tarbert is credited with the sum of £4 8s 10d, as the "Contributio pacis" of the burgh. This appears to have been a contribution towards the amount which Scotland was called upon to pay to England as a war indemnity by the terms of the treaty of Northampton.

While little indication of the extent or population can be gathered from the fact of its being a royal burgh, it may be reasonably inferred that even at this early date a community of considerable size must have existed in the village and its immediate neighbourhood.

The following extract from a "Report on the settlement of the Revenues of Excise and Customs in Scotland," submitted to the Government more than three centuries later, viz, in 1656, by a Mr Thomas Tucker, is of much interest in connection with the position of Tarbert as a place of export, and the early methods of communication between the Western Islands and the centres of trade, as well as from its giving an indication of the class of mercandize which the Highlanders of the seventeenth century brought to market. Although there are a few discrepances, there can be no doubt the reference is to Tarbert, both from the fact of the method described having been, as is well known, largely employed at this isthmus, and from its being the only place on Lochfyne to which the description otherwise could apply. The extract is as follows :—

The inhabitants of Glasgow trade and deal "with their neighbours the Highlanders who come hither from the Isles and westerne parts; in summer by the Mul of Cantyre, and in winter by the Torban to the head (should be mouth) of Loquh Fyn (which is a small neck of sandy land, over which they usually draive their small boats into the Firth of Dunbarton), and soe passe up in the Cluyde with pladding, dry hides, goate, kid and deer skyns, which they sell, and purchase with theyr price such comodityes and provisions as they stand in neede of from time to time."

With reference to the practice of dragging boats between the two lochs, Pennant in his "Tour in Scotland" remarks:—"It is not very long since vessels of nine or ten tuns were drawn by horses out of the west loch into that of the east, to avoid the dangers of the Mull of Cantyre, so dreaded and so little known was the navigation round that promontory."

CHAPTER III.

FROM the year 1335, the date of the Earl of Moray's sojourn in the castle, till 1494, when James IV. was king, history is silent regarding Tarbert and its affairs. In this year we discover distinct traces of a royal visit.

For many years previously the clan feuds which distracted Kintyre and the western islands proved a source of extreme annoyance to the Scottish crown, and the attempts made to settle contending claims were as frequent as they were unavailing.

In the year 1493, James IV. visited Campbeltown, and, to quote from the "Pictorial History of Scotland," "in the course of the year 1494 he visited the Isles no fewer than three times, so great was his anxiety to establish the authority of law and government in these remote districts."

On two of these occasions, at least, James resided

at Tarbert for a time. During his first visit, which occurred in April, he made extensive repairs on the castle, and, as showing the importance he attached to it, he provided it, at this early period in the history of firearms, "with artillery and skilful gunners."

To this visit Tytler refers in the following terms :—" At Tarbert, in Kintyre, he repaired the fort originally built by Bruce, and established an emporium for his shipping, transporting thither his artillery, laying in a stock of gunpowder, and carrying along with him his master gunners, in whose training and practice he appears, from the payments in the treasurer's books, to have busied himself with much perseverance and enthusiasm."

In the month of July King James is again at Tarbert. This occasion is rendered somewhat memorable by the fact that Parliament was summoned to meet him there in order to deliberate on the means to be employed for securing a more settled state of affairs in Kintyre and the Southern Isles.

Regarding this meeting we learn from the preface to Vol. I. of the accounts of the Lord High Treasurer that " on the 5th of July, 1494, the lords of the east, south, and west were summoned to meet King James IV. at Tarbert, where, accordingly, we find him on the twenty-fourth with the Christopher and other ships, gunners and munitions of war. Having repaired the castle of Tarbert, and victualled and garrisoned it as a basis of operations, he proceeded to reduce the castle of Dunaverty, in South Kintyre."

The expenses connected with the summoning of the Lords at this time, and the method by which it was effected, are gathered from the two following entries in the Treasurer's accounts:—"In primis the V day of Julü, gevin to Donald Malynne, currour, to pass with letters to the Lords of the Westland for the meeting of the King at the Terbert, xs (10s)."   "Item to John Keir to pass with sic lik letters in the Southland and the Eastland, xiiijs."

As illustrating the King's generosity and the habits of the times, the following entry is interesting and significant:—"Item gevin to the gunnaris, the.xxiiij day of Julü, be the King's command, to drinksilver, xls (40s)."

Nor were the necessities of the chapel overlooked, for mention is made of £6 13s 4d having been given towards its expenses "quhen the King was at the Terbert."

In the accounts of this year, also, we find the Bishop of Dunblane credited with having forwarded £20 "to the bigin of Tarbert," and a like sum was "resauit fra the Abbot of Newbotill for the said caus."

The next occasion on which we find King James at Tarbert was in the year 1498.   It is thus referred to in the preface just quoted from:—"He sailed

on the 8th of March (from Ayr), and touching at
Arran, proceeded to the new castle which he had
built at the head of Loch Kilkerane, now Campbeltown, in South Kintyre. Having spent a week
there and at Tarbert, he returned by way of Ayr
to Duchal." "Desirous of providing for the strong-
holds he had established there and at Tarbert, he
sometime after sent 'ane cole man to pas in Kintyre
to vesy gif colis may be wonnyne thare.'" Following this entry in the accounts of the period is one
of eighteen shillings paid to a Dumbarton collier
to make working tools and proceed into Kintyre.

The reader of Scottish history needs not to be
informed that notwithstanding the frequent efforts
then made for the pacification of the rival clans,
Kintyre and the Southern Hebrides continued in
a state of lawlessness and bloodshed. In April,
1499, we therefore find this able and energetic
monarch once more at Tarbert.

About this time a new policy began to be adopted
for the enforcement of order among the clans in
the more seriously disturbed districts, and in the
course of this year we find the Government applying it to the districts around Tarbert. This policy
consisted in the giving of grants of lands, castles,
&c., to some of the more powerful nobles, in return
for which they were bound to maintain order in
their respective districts.

From the fact of the clan Campbell being one of
the most powerful in Argyllshire, and the most

likely from this and other circumstances to curb
the turbulence of other clans, this position was
assigned to them in several parts of the shire.
According to Gregory, the influence of the Argyll
family was first brought to bear on Kintyre and
the Isles in the following manner:—

During the visit of James IV., which has just
been referred to, "he gave a commission to Archibald, Earl of Argyll, and others, for letting on
lease for the term of three years, the entire lordship of the Isles, as possessed by the last lord both
in the Isles and on the mainland, excepting only
the Island of Isla, and the lands of North and
South Kintyre. Argyll received also a commission
of lieutenandry, with the fullest powers over the
lordship of the Isles."

A few months later he was appointed "Keeper
of the castle of Tarbert, with the 'balyery and
governans' of the lands of Knapdale and all profits
and dues belonging to the same, to be held during
the King's pleasure."

But these concessions were only the introduction.
In 1505 there was further "granted to the same
earl the offices of Justiciar and Chamberlain of
the lands and lordships of Knapdaill and Kintyre,
and of Captain of the house and fortalice of Tarbert, and also the lands of Kilberry and the south
half of Knapdaill, with the patronage of the church
of Kilberry (all united into the barony of Tarbert),
with one half of the King's dues." In the years

1526, 1529, 1541, and 1542, the grant in one form or other was renewed and confirmed, the influence of the Argylls in the neighbourhood increased and strengthened, and the keeping of the castle of Tarbert has ever since remained in the hands of the family of MacCalein Mor as the feudal superiors.

Among the many changes of ownership which the lands in the neighbourhood of Tarbert had undergone from one cause or other previous to this date, it is difficult to trace the proprietorship connectedly. In the thirteenth century, and for some centuries later, Tarbert, and much of the north of Kintyre, formed part of the barony or lordship of Knapdale. Early in the thirteenth century most of Knapdale, including the lands of Skipness, and those in the neighbourhood of Clachan, seem to have been possessed by Syfyn or Swene of Argyll. As early as 1262 Dufgal the son of Swene granted to Walter Steward, "Earl of Menthet," his land of Skipness reaching over the country to Clachan, "in free barony for payment to the King of two-thirds of the service of one soldier and other services." At some time previous to the year 1310, Robert Bruce is said to have granted Knapdale to John of Menthet, a descendant of the above Walter Steward, but in this year "King Edward II. of England, in order that John the son of Swien of Argyll, and Terrealnanogh and Murquocgh his brothers might render them-

selves more hateful to John of Meneteth, his
enemy, and to others his enemies in Scotland,
granted to them the whole land of Knapdale which
belonged to their ancestors, provided they could
recover it out of his enemies' hands." In this
extract we have an interesting illustration of one
of the methods employed by the English for
increasing their influence and furthering their ends
even in these remote districts.

From the Origines Parochiales we learn further
that :—" In the year 1335, Edward Balliol granted
to John of the Isles for his allegiance ' the land of
Knappedoll' and other lands." This was the period
when the Earl of Moray visited Tarbert, in order to
negotiate with the Lord of the Isles, who was said
by the Scottish historian "to favour the English
interest."

" In 1376, King Robert II granted to John Del
Yle, and Margaret, his wife, half of his lands in
Knapdale."

" In 1475, John, Earl of Ross, and Lord of the
Isles, forfeited all his possessions to the crown, and
on his restoration in 1476, the lordship of Knapdale
was reserved to the crown."

In 1481, King James III. seems to have restored
to them all the more modern lordship of Knapdale,
which, however, it is noted, was claimed by
"Makelane and Maknele." Most of the places
mentioned in this grant will yet be known from
their old spelling. They are as follows :—Barm ore

Garalane, Achnafey, Strondowr, Glenmolane, Glen-
raole, Largbanan, Barnellane, Kowildrinoch, Glan-
nafeoch, Ardpatrik, Ardmenys, Largnahowshyn,
Forleyngloch, Crevyr, Drumnamwkloch, Kilmalo-
wok, Drumdrisok, Schengart, Bargawre, Clachbrek,
Balonkyrt, Arrymore, Owragaig, Achtydownegall,
Scottomyl, Drummalaycht, Downynskeig, Le Lowb,
Lemnamwk, Gartwaiche, Tescard, Altbeith, Crag-
keith, Achetymalane, Dowynynvltoch, Renochane,
Kilchamok, Gartnagruach, and Ormisay. The
Knapdale portion of the district covered by these
names, as distinguished from the Kintyre part, was
included in the Commission granted to the Earl of
Argyll in 1499.

CHAPTER IV.

A FREEBOOTER OF THE OLDEN TIMES.

BY an historian of the sixteenth century, a rather black picture is presented of the morals and manners of the Islesmen of those days. Indeed, they would seem to have been little removed from barbarism. "The Highlanders who dwell on the mainland, though sufficiently wild," he allows, "show some shade of civilisation; but those in the islands are without laws or morals, and totally destitute of religion and humanity." The many stories that exist of feuds conducted with savage cruelty, demonstrate only too plainly that the general accusation was not unwarranted. Freebooting and piracy were rampant. These were the days in which Alan-nan-Sop, one of the most noted pirates and freebooters that the Scottish coast has ever produced, was at the height of his power, and he, along with many others of like predatory tendencies, succeeded effectually in keeping all the western parts in a state of ferment and terror.

This Alan was an illegitimate son of Lachlan Catanach MacLean, of Duart, chief of the clan MacLean, by a daughter of the laird of Tresinish. According to some, his nick-name of Alan-nan-Sop (Alan of the Straw) was derived from his having been born, by some accident, on a heap of straw, while according to others he received it in consequence of a custom he had of setting fire to houses with his own hand, by means of a blazing wisp of straw, when on his freebooting expeditions.

Some years after the birth of Alan, the beauty of his mother having captivated MacLean of Torloisk, a man of rank in the clan, he married her and took her to reside at his castle of Torloisk.

Unfortunately for Alan, or rather for many others who suffered in consequence, he succeeded in securing his step-father's ill-will. He was therefore forced to shift for himself, and strive by some means or other to win an inheritance independently of the old chieftain. Young, strong, and brave to desperation, he entered as a sailor on board one of the numerous ships engaged in piracy along the coast, and " in process of time obtained the command, first of one galley, then of a small flotilla, with which he sailed round the seas and collected considerable plunder, until his name became both feared and famous."

From the following translation of a paper which
appeared in a Gaelic magazine, "Cuairtear Nan
Gleann," of August, 1841, it will be observed that
Alan resided for a time in the Castle of Tarbert,
and had considerable possessions in the neighbourhood.   On account of previous writers having
circulated many untruths regarding the redoubtable
Alan, to the regret of the author of this paper, he
announces his effort as being an earnest attempt to
give a true and faithful account of the doings of his
hero, and we may accept it as such.   Regarding
the statement contained therein with reference to
the gift of Tarbert Castle by MacDonald of Islay,
we may suppose he received it from the latter for
the taking of it from his hereditary enemies, the
Campbells.   Once in his possession, Argyll evidently preferred to have him as a friend than a foe.
That part of the paper which refers more particularly to Tarbert is as follows :—

"There is nothing which shows more plainly the cunning
and might of this man than the fact that MacDonald of
Islay bought his friendship by giving him as an estate the
island of Gigha and villages at the head of Loch Tarbert.
This warrior or robber spent much time in the Castle of
Tarbert, which he obtained from MacDonald; and M'Cailein
Mor bought his friendship by giving him an estate in Knap-
dale, a fertile region called Kilcharmaig.

By the friendship of these great men, MacCailein,
MacDonald, and his brother, Hector Mor of Duart, Ailean-
nan-Sop was exceedingly powerful, and became a cause of
terror to his enemies, but, although he possessed so many
valuable estates, he did not cease plundering and destroying.
From Tarbert Castle he used to go to Cowal, and to Loch

Lomond side, and through the country of the Lowlands, carrying off booty from every place. He used also to go with ships to Ireland, burning, and destroying, and carrying off plunder, so that Ailean-nan-Sop was as well known in Ireland as he was in Scotland. He went once to collect spoil from the Isle of Bute ; the sheriff heard that he was coming, and gathered his men, but they could not withstand the bold warriors who were with Alan ; he brought away a shipful of cattle, the best that he could get.

Alan's conduct caused great sorrow to that high-minded and honorable man, Hector Mor, his brother, and to his kinsman, the Lord of Coll. Alan heard something that the Lord of Coll had said against him, and he set off to Coll to take vengeance on him. The Lord of Coll was walking on the shore ; Alan laid hold of him, and took him on board his boat, made him prisoner, and tied him to a rower's bench, hoisted his sail, and set off to Tarbert.

The Lord of Coll was a noted bard, and he began to make a song to Ailean-nan-Sop. He sang the song—this got the better of Alan—he loosed him and gave him his freedom, saying to him, "Take care what you say about me after this—there is a little bird in Coll that comes to tell me your language at your own table—I will let you go, but be on your guard henceforth." (Thoir an aire ciod a their thu 'na dhèigh so mu m' thimchioll-sa—tha eun beag ann an Cola tha tighin a dh' innseadh dhòmhsa do chainnt aig do bhòrd fèin—leigidh mi as thu, ach bi a' d' earalas à so a mach.)

When Alan became old, he gave up his evil habits, and abandoned plundering and robbing, but this did not please his warriors who were in the castle—the flesh was not so plentiful as it used to be. On a certain day he gave a feast, and one of his men was picking a bone on which there was not much to be got. "A wonderful change has come on this house," said he, "when the bones are so bare." ("'Sann air an tigh so," ars 'esan, "a thainig an dá latha 'nuair tha na cnámhan co lom") Alan heard him, and understood what was meant—"Let every boat that belongs to us be ready to-night, our boys and our men, and we will try to put in a little flesh for the winter." (Biodh gach birlinn a bhuineas duinn deas an nochd, ar gillean 's ar daoine, agus fiachaidh sinn beagan feóla chur a stigh air son a' gheamhraidh.) Off they set through the Kyles of Bute, and went up the river Clyde to near Glasgow ; they took much spoil, and returned with every boat filled. This is the greatest and the last booty that Ailean-nan-Sop every took, and he gave it the name of the "spoil of the rib" (in allusion to the bone which his follower had been picking.)

Alan became very aged. He went to Icolmkill, and made his peace with the clergy, and shortly afterwards died, and was buried in Iona in St. Oran's burying ground with his ancestors, the family of Duart.

Alan had one son and one daughter. He put his son to death because he attempted to murder Hector Mor, his father's brother ; and his daughter married Murdoch the Short, of Lochbuy. The estate that Alan took from the "Family of the Iron Sword," the family of Leitir, came after his death to MacLean of Duart, and he gave it to Lachlan Og, son of Sir Lachlan Mor of Duart, and from him came the family of Torloisk.

Ailean-nan-Sop died about the year 1555, between that and 1560, The flat stone on this man's grave can be discovered in Icolmkill."

CHAPTER V.

THE SHERIFFDOM OF TARBERT.

IN such lawless and turbulent times as those we have been referring to, the difficulty in administering the law was in no district felt to such an extent as in that embraced in the present shire of Argyll. The large area which it covers, the diversified character of the country, and the inclusion within it of so many islands, would indeed at that time have made the task an almost impossible one. As a result of this, we find that at the period we have been referring to, the northern portions were attached to the shire of Inverness, the central and larger portion of the mainland constituted the Sheriffdom of Lorne or Argyll, and the remainder was formed into the shire or Sheriffdom of Tarbert. Regarding the date of formation of the shire of Tarbert, it cannot be arrived at, but its existence may be traced as far back as the year 1481.

Including as it did within its jurisdiction the districts of Kintyre and Knapdale, the islands of Gigha, Islay, Jura, Scarba, Colonsay, and Mull, together with a number of the smaller isles, its extent was very considerable.

It is somewhat peculiar to find that previous to 26th February, 1481, when it was made a part of the shire of Tarbert, the district of Knapdale was included in the shire of Perth. At an earlier period still, however, it formed a portion of the shire of Lorn or Argyll.

The hereditary offices connected with the shire of Tarbert were for the greater part of its existence held by the house of Argyll. Among these offices were those of Heritable Lieutenant, Chamberlain, Sheriff, and Coroner.

Until its amalgamation (when the country was more settled) with the shire of Argyll in 1633, in accordance with an Act of Parliament passed on 28th June of that year, it continued to send up its representative to Parliament, its last member being Sir Lachlan M'Lean, of Morvern, who had been elected by the Freeholders in September, 1628.

The following extract from the Act by which it was abolished is of considerable interest:—

" His Majestie with advyse and consent of the thrie estates of this present Parliament, Hes united and be thir presents unites The said shirefdome of Tarbett to the forsaid shirefdome of Argyll, And ordaines baith the saids shirefdoms of Argyll and Tarbett heirby united as said is To be callit in all tyme coming the shirefdome of Argyll." And further, it goes on to add that "no citationes, sumonds, denunciationes of hornings, inhibitiones, brieves, nor na uther sick publick citations or proclamationes sall be usit at na tyme heireftir at the mercatt croce or accustomat place of Tarbett."

It appears that during a portion at least of the period of its existence, the law officers of the shire of Tarbert were unable to overtake the work committed to them, for we find that by an Act of Parliament passed in 1503, a Sheriff was specially appointed for the " south Ilis and thai partis," who was to have his seat either at Tarbert or Loch Kilkerran. The following extract from the Act explains fully the reasons for the new appointment :

"Item becaus thair hes bene greit abusioun of Justice in the northt partis and west partis of the realme, sic as the northt Ilis and south Ilis, for lak and falt of Justiceairis Justicis, and schirefis And thairthrou the pepill ar almaist gane wild It is thairfor statute and ordainit for the acquietting of the pepill be Justice that thair be in tyme to cum Justicis and schirefis depute in thai partis as eftir folowis that is to say That the Justicis and schirefis of the northt Ilis haif thair sait and place for administratioun of Justice in Invernes or Dingwale as the materis occurris to be decernyt be the saidis officiaris And that ane uther Justice and schiref be maid and depute for the south Ilis and thai partis and to haif his place and sait for administratioun of Justice in the tarbart or at lochkinkerane at the will and plesour of the saidis officiaris as the materis occurris."

Although for administrative purposes the separate existence of the shire of Tarbert ceased in 1633, the frequency with which the phrase "Shire of Tarbert" occurs for many years afterwards in proclamations, letters, &c., shows that for practical purposes such

as the massing of levies, the sub-division was felt
to be very convenient. It is not till the year 1705
that we find the expression " Tarbet in the shire of
Argyll," occurring in the records.

A somewhat thorough search through the " Acts
of the Parliaments of Scotland," and the " Register
of the Privy Council," has been productive of a few
items of information which serve to act as land-
marks in the history of Tarbert and its shire, and
to link it, in some instances slightly, in others to
an important extent, with the most stirring events
of the times.

These were the days in the history of our country
when every man was more or less a soldier, and
ready, at any time, to don his armour and assume
his weapons at the call of his superior or chief.
Taking advantage of such a condition of affairs,
Government determined to find means of improving
the fighting power of the nation, and bringing it
more under the control of the central authority,
and with this end in view an Act was passed on
5th March, 1574, entitled an Act " Anent the
making of Wapinschawingis." In stating its purport
and necessity it declares that " forasmekle as it is
maist requisite that in time of peace provision be
maid and cair taken for the weare when at goddis
pleasur it may happen," wappinschaws should be
held twice a year (on July 20th and October 10th)
at convenient places within the several jurisdictions.

This was the nearest approach to the compulsory system of the Continent that our country has ever adopted. All able-bodied men were required, on penalty of a fine, to attend these gatherings at the proper time and place, provided with weapons and armour suitable to the rank of the individual, and they were held on the same day all over the country, lest the same weapons, &c., should be made use of by different persons, thus leading to a deficiency which could only be discovered when they were called out for active service.

In order that the Government might have a thorough knowledge of the military capabilities of each district, the Sheriffs, Bailies, &c., were ordered to send a complete list of the muster and of the weapons to the Regent, within forty days after the Wappinschaw, under a penalty of one hundred marks. Certain persons were appointed to co-operate with the above officers in receiving the musters, examining the arms, &c., and we find that those who were commissioned at this time to act in the Sheriffdom of Tarbert were James Campbell, of Ardkinglas, and Dugald Campbell, of Auchinbreck.

Probably as a result of these grand field days and the increased control thus gained over the clans, levies from the outlying districts came to be more frequently employed for imperial purposes in other and distant parts of the country. In the year 1579 we find that a levy of all the inhabitants

within the shire of Tarbert was ordered for service
at the siege of the castles of Hamilton and Draffen,
held by the Hamilton's against the King. In 1580,
1582, and 1588, levies were raised for employment
against the Border thieves; in 1584, against the
"enemies of the true religion in the North;" in
1592 and 1601, against the M'Gregors; and in
1596 and 1608, against the Islesmen.

In the year 1597 they were for the fourth time
called upon for service against the Border thieves,
but on this occasion the levy partook of the nature
of a compromise, as expressed in the proclamation,
when it states it to be lawful to the "haill inhabitants of Tarbett, comprehending thairin Ergyll," to
furnish "ane hundreth hieland men with a commander bodin with hacquetbutis, bowis, havirshonis,
swerdis, darlochis, and targeis," and that the obser-
vance of this alternative by the said sheriffdom
"sall releve the haill remanent inhabitants thairof
fra thair personal service to this present raid."

In 1581, a sum of £40,000 (Scots) was granted
by Parliament for the purpose of repressing the
Border thieves, and resisting a threatened English
invasion, which sum was to be raised by a special
tax. In the following year, Colin, Earl of Argyll,
was sued for non-payment of the portion imposed
on the shire of Tarbert, and in the course of a
petition to the Privy Council to stay the letters of
horning against him, the following passage occurs.
It demonstrates very plainly how unaccustomed

the Highlanders of these days were to taxation, and how little inclined they were to at all acknowledge the principle of sharing the burdens of the State :—

" Attoure, gif the said compliner in onywyse be addettit in the said taxatioun, the samin is only as schiref of the schirefdome of Tarbert ; quhilk hes nevir bene in use of paying ony taxatioun or contributioun in ony King's tyme of befoir : yea scarslie will pay thair awin few males,—the saidis haill landis, at the leist for the maist part, nevir being stentit nor retourit, yea the maist part of the samin bruikit but sesing or evident ; and the farthest the said compliner can be addettit into is bot only to do his diligence. Quhilk he hes done already : viz upoun lettirs of impetrat be him of his Hienes and the saidis Lordis of Secrete Counsale, he hes causit charge the frehalders, under the pane of rebellioun, to mak payment, lyke as alswa he wald have causit poind thair reddiest guidis and geir for the samin."

The Privy Council commanded Argyll to pay the sum by a certain date, or else " to report lettirs dewlie execute and indorsat upoun the barronis, frehalders, and utheris, addettit in payment thairof," and in the meantime suspended the letters of horning.

CHAPTER VI.

MILITARY AFFAIRS, 1600-1745.

THE seventeenth century had scarcely dawned ere James VI., in one of his more courageous moods, made the brave resolve of undertaking an expedition in person to Kintyre and the Isles, in order to bring his rebellious subjects of these regions to submission. Accordingly we find a proclamation was issued in April, 1600, commanding the inhabitants of the shires of Ayr, Renfrew, Dumbarton, and some other districts, to meet him at Dumbarton on the 10th of July. Two days after this date he hoped to reach Tarbert, where all within the bounds of Tarbert, Bute, Argyll, Athole, and Breadalbane, were instructed to await his arrival.

In order that their passage to the Isles might be facilitated, all the boatmen and ferriers upon the water of Clyde and the whole sea-coast thereabout were summoned to repair to the "ferry of Tarbett" (evidently Port 'a Mhaidhe, on the Kerry shore), with their boats upon the said 12th July, and there attend for transporting the army under pain of loss of life, lands, and goods.

Arrived at Tarbert, we can readily picture the boats conveyed across the isthmus as on the occasions made memorable by former royal progresses; and once upon the waters of the Western Loch, a few hours sail would suffice to transport them, it might be, to the south of Kintyre, to Islay's verdant shore, or other disaffected district.

At the last moment, however, the projected expedition was abandoned, firstly on account of the poverty and distress of the people of Scotland at that time, and secondly, for what would probably appear to James the more important reason, viz., that he was afraid to "hasard himselff" there unless well supported by troops.

Several years after the collapse of this well-intentioned project, the old system introduced in the fifteenth century for the quieting of turbulent districts was again had recourse to.

In Kintyre and the Southern Isles the chief disturbing influence continued to be the Macdonald's, and the several offshoots of that ancient and powerful clan. That their power should be curbed if peace was to be secured and civilisation fostered, seemed to the Government of the day an absolute necessity, and no more convenient or less expensive method could be devised than that of setting one powerful clan against another by holding out the temptation of increased territory.

Accordingly, in the year 1607, the grants formerly referred to as having been made to the Argyll family in the neighbourhood of Tarbert were so far extended as to include the whole of Kintyre.

That the brave descendants of the Lords of the Isles should tamely submit to this wholesale deprivation of their choicest possessions was not for a moment to be expected, and the years of petty though bloody warfare that ensued between the two clans only ceased when in the year 1615 the power of the Macdonald's was effectually broken.

For twelve years previous to this date their chief, Sir James Macdonald, was a prisoner in Edinburgh, and during six of these years he lay under sentence of death. In the spring of this year, however, he succeeded in effecting his escape, and sought the shelter of the Isles as speedily as possible. Once more restored to the land of his forefathers, his position as chief was soon realised, and he very shortly found himself at the head of a body of four hundred men, mostly natives of the northern isles.

Knowing full well the restless nature of the clan, and feeling assured that an effort of a determined character would now be made, the Government, in the absence of Argyll in England, gave orders to Sir D. Campbell, of Auchinbreck, and Campbell of Ardkinglas, to take measures for the protection of

Argyll proper, Knapdale and Kintyre.   Until the
Earl should arrive, Auchinbreck was appointed to
the chief command, and the men of Tarbert,
Argyll, Ayr, Dumbarton, Renfrew, &c., were under
orders to attend him when required.

As was anticipated, Sir James was not long
inactive.   Having completed some fortifications in
Islay, he forthwith landed on the shores of Kintyre,
and sent the fiery cross throughout that district to
summon all the Macdonalds to arms.

Towards the end of July he moved northwards
in full force, and took up a position about ten
miles from Tarbert, announcing his determination
to reach the isthmus about the thirtieth of the
month.

Auchinbreck by this time, however, had gathered
to him three hundred men with whom he held the
isthmus, his object being simply to prevent the
Macdonalds from leaving Kintyre and pushing
into Knapdale.   In this resolve he was confirmed
by the Government, who, though ordering Ardkin-
glass and Lochnell to join him with the men of
Cowal and Lorn, impressed upon him the desirableness of not risking an attack, but of simply con-
tenting himself with holding his position, and
confining the Macdonalds to the peninsula till the
arrival of Argyll.   In this manner the Macdonalds,
who do not appear to have shown much activity,
were cooped up in Kintyre during the whole of
August.

In the following month Argyll arrived upon the scene. At Duntroon, on Loch Crinan, he mustered his forces, having among them a contingent of four hundred hired soldiers, whom he had received from the Government. Few of the men of the shire of Tarbert having joined Argyll from the fact of their being nearly all Macdonalds or favourers of the clan, the employment of these mercenaries was rendered all the more necessary.

The Earl's course of action was soon determined upon. Having ascertained that Macdonald's galleys were stationed at the island of Cara, he decided on surprising them, if possible, by night, with the view of lessening their chances of escape from the mainland, and with this intent despatched Calder with a fleet of galleys containing a force of eight hundred men. On the same day he himself reached Tarbert with the remainder of the troops, where they were joined to those under the command of Auchinbreck.

It was high time for Sir James to bestir himself. Advised of the arrival of Argyll, and determined, if possible, to prevent his advance into Kintyre, he hurried forward his Uncle Ranald with from three to four hundred men, "to stop the passage from Tarbert on the east," whilst Coll MacGillespick (Coll Ciotach) with three boats and sixty men proceeded to West Tarbert to reconnoitre.

Coll had the first stroke of success. Campbell of Kilberry being engaged on a like service on the side of Argyll, he and some of his followers were captured by Coll, who then retreated, intending to make for the ships at Cara with his prisoners. By this time, however, Calder had reached Gigha, and Coll, still retaining the captives, found himself obliged to hasten to Kintyre, and abandon his boats. Notwithstanding Calder's arrival at Gigha, he was unsuccessful in the object of his cruise, Keppoch and the others who had been left with the ships having been warned of the approach of the ships of Argyll by a beacon which Largie's people had lighted, and so made good their escape. Their flight, however, was a serious and unexpected shock to Sir James.

On the east side, also, misfortune awaited the Macdonalds. Attacked by Argyll, they were forced to yield, and beat a hasty retreat. Though pursued far into Kintyre they succeeded in effecting their escape, but were so cut up that Sir James was compelled to leave the peninsula, and seek a shelter in Rachrin. Later on the unfortunate chief returned to Islay, then passed over to Ireland, and finally left the British Isles and sought a safe refuge in Spain.

Keppoch and some of the other officers secured a safe retreat in Ireland. Coll Ciotach found his way to Islay, where for a time he held out in two forts, but finally surrendered, and afterwards becoming an active partisan of Argyll, he captured and delivered up to the authorities Macfie of Colonsay and eighteen others of his old allies.

By the beginning of November the insurrection was completely quelled, and Argyll received orders to disband his hired troops. For some reason or other, however, he retained them for a period of six weeks longer, a proceeding which (more particularly as all the chiefs of the rebellion had escaped), nearly led to his incurring severe censure. As it was, the Government compelled him to pay out of his own resources the soldiers' allowances for those six weeks.

Though thus effectually humbled for a time, it was not long ere the Macdonalds were again able to take the field in force. Eighteen months after the crushing defeat of Montrose at Philiphaugh, the only chief remaining in arms for the king in the south and west was Sir Alister Macdonald, of Dunaverty, son of the brave Coll Ciotach. With over a thousand men he so ravaged Kintyre that in May, 1647, General David Lesley and the Marquis of Argyll advanced with the covenanting forces in order to expel him from the district. As illustrating the ease with which at that time it was felt the isthmus of Tarbert might be held against any army endeavouring to enter Kintyre from the Knapdale side, the following letter may be quoted. It is from the pen of Sir James Turner, Adjutant-General of this little army, and runs thus :—" From Inveraray we marched to Kintyre, which is a peninsula. Both before and at the entry to it, there were such advantages of ground that our foot for

mountains and marshes could never have drawn
up one hundred in a body, nor our horse above
three in a breast, which, if Sir Alister had pre-
possessed with those thousand or twelve hundred
brave foot that he had with him, I think he might
have ruined us, at least we should not have entered
Kintyre (but by a miracle);" and then in the true
covenanter strain he goes on to add, " but he was
ordained for destruction, for, by a speedy march, we
made ourselves masters of these difficult passes, and
got into a plain country, where ńo sooner he saw
our horse advance, but with little or no fighting he
retired.

The result of the expedition, the defeat of Sir
Alister at Runaherin, his retreat to the Castle of
Dunaverty, and the ultimate fate of its garrison, are
well known matters of Highland history.

During the period of the Commonwealth, Tarbert
Castle, in common with most of the castles in
Scotland, passed into the possession of the Roundheads, by whom it is stated to have been strengthened by the construction of bastions and outworks.

The following note of how it was re-captured by
a body of Tarbert men is taken from Aikman's
continuation of George Buchanan's history.   After
referring to the fact of Argyll's having been surprised
by some Parliamentary forces while he lay ill at
Inverary, of his having reluctantly submitted to the
Commonwealth, and accompanied their forces to

Dumbarton, as well as to the fact that some of his vassals, thinking, or pretending to think, that on his way thither he was a prisoner, stopped their march through a certain defile, he proceeds: "Others seized the castle of Tarbert on the same pretext during the absence of the greater part of the garrison, who had gone a-nutting, from which they took ten barrels of gunpowder, five thousand weight of cheese, and twenty-six bags of biscuit: for this, however, they afterwards made an apology to the major-general, who politically accepted it, and not being too rigid in requiring restitution, his forces were treated with more kindness in that district, and their officers entertained at the expense of Argyll, whose interests demanded that he should use them with hospitality, when further hostility would only have aggravated his irremediable ruin."

From a contemporary, Sir Bulstrode Whitelocke, we learn that the above incident occurred about the beginning of September, 1652, and that the officer who was in command of the garrison at the time of the surrender was a Lieutenant Gillot.

Eight years from the above date, the Commonwealth had ceased to be, Charles II. was restored to the throne whose privileges he had abused; the great Marquis of Argyll, to whom we have just referred, and who had placed the crown on the King's head at Scone, was speedily brought to the block, and some years afterwards his son, the Earl of Argyll, was condemned to death, but escaped into exile before the bloody deed could be committed. After the discovery of the Rye-house plot in England, measures were taken to prevent a rising in the Campbell country, from the fact that the exiled Earl was stated to have promised aid to the conspirators, by calling his clansmen to arms against the Government in Scotland.

That the measures were of a very thorough nature will be inferred from the fact that Charles appointed six lieutenants of the " shires of Argyll and Tarbet," who were called the lieutenants of Cowal, Inverary, " Sadel " or Kintyre, " Craigness," Dunstaffnage, and Tarbet respectively, and further issued a royal proclamation on May 5th, 1684, in which he commanded certain nobles and gentlemen to "have in Readiness with all convenient Diligence the respective Proportions and Number of Men aftermentioned, well provided in Feir of Weir, well armed, and with Thirty Days Provision, for concurring with and assisting our said Lieutenants, &c."

The noblemen and gentlemen who were instructed to come to the assistance of the Lieutenant of Tarbert, and the number of men they were respectively to bring, were as follows :—" The Earl of Mar Three Hundred Men, the Laird of Weem One Hundred Men, the Earl of Seaforth Three Hundred Men, and Sir Donald M'Donald of Slait Two Hundred Men," while " all in the shires of

Aberdeen, and Banff above Kincardine of Neil, Kildrummy, and Keith," were also to answer the Lieutenant of Tarbert, and be ready to come to his assistance on six days' warning, with thirty days' provision.

The preparations, however, were at this time unnecessary, the country remaining undisturbed.

With the events of the following year the history of Tarbert is intimately associated. Charles had died, and was succeeded in February of 1685 by James the seventh of Scotland and second of England.

In the spring of this year Argyll, with several influential covenanters who also had taken refuge in Holland, resolved on an invasion of Scotland, in order to wrest his native country from the rule of a Popish king. In conjunction with this effort the unhappy Duke of Monmouth made his unsuccessful attempt in the south.

It being anticipated that the landing in Scotland would be effected in some part of the Earl's territory, with a view to making preparations for the invasion, the Marquis of Athole on April 29th received a commission as Lord Lieutenant of the "shires of Argyll and Tarbert."

With the command of the expedition Argyll was nominally, but only nominally entrusted, for even before they left Holland, the Lowland refugees set themselves diligently to devise means of limiting his power, and of controlling all the movements

of their so-called leader. Having touched at Kirk-
wall and Islay on their way, the expedition reached
Campbeltown after a prosperous voyage, and there
the Earl printed and dispersed a Declaration of
War against the King, which had been prepared in
Holland by a namesake of His Majesty, James
Stuart, an " eminent lawyer and excellent person."
Soon the fiery cross was hurried over hill and dale
to summon to arms all the Campbells from sixteen
to sixty, and the isthmus of Tarbert, " a very centrical place," was fixed as the rendezvous. Slowly
the summons was obeyed, and those who did
appear seemed impelled more with love to the long
banished Earl than with fondness for the cause.
Encouraging accounts having been received from
the Lowlands, Sir John Cochrane, Sir Patrick
Hume, and others "ernestly pressed the Erle that
wee might divide, and some of us go thither; he
seemed satisfied, but withal, told us that his son
Charles and other gentlemen were at Tarbot-Castle
with 1200 men, and if we would saile the ships
thither, and many boats wee had, he with Sir John
(Cochrane) and a good pairt of the sogers, would
take a land march through Kantire, levie the whole
country, and joine them, and that we might then
goe to the Lowlands with a considerable division
of men   .   .   .   .   So he marched, and
we sailed ; came to Tarbot, and found our friends
at a rendezvous here. We made of horse and foot
1800 men."

The date of arrival at Tarbert was 27th May, and here the Earl printed a declaration concerning himself, in which, after rebutting the assertion of his enemies that this expedition was simply undertaken in order to recover his own lands, and expressing his grief at his "former too much complying with and conniving at the Methods" which had brought so much evil on his country, he goes on to state his purpose boldly thus:—" I have now with God's Strength suffered patiently my unjust Sentence and Banishment, Three Years and an Half, and never offered to make any Uprore or Defence by Arms, to disturb the peace upon my private Concern; but the King being now dead, and the Duke of York having taken off his Mask, and having abandoned and invaded our Religion and Liberties, resolving to enter into the Government and exercise it contrary to Law, I think it is not only just, but my Duty to God and my Country, to use my utmost Endeavours to oppose and repress his Usurpation and Tyranny; and therefore being assisted and furnished very nobly by several good Protestants, and invited, and accompanied by several of both Nations, to lead them, I resolve, as God shall enable me to use their Assistance of all kind toward the ends expressed in the said Declaration (The Declaration of War), I do earnestly invite and obtest all honest Protestants and particularly all my Friends and blood Relations to concur with us in the said Undertaking," &c., &c.

These were brave words, but the time was when they would have been backed up by greater strength of arms than on this occasion answered to the Earl's summons. In earlier and more prosperous times, instead of the 1800 men that assembled at Tarbert, a MacCalein Mor could have easily raised 5000 or 6000 claymores; but so many chieftains had been thrown into prison, and so much had their territories been ravaged, that the spirit of the clan Campbell was broken.

Nothing daunted, however, the Earl proceeded to organise his forces. The horse were placed under Rumbold's command, while the infantry were divided into three regiments from 500 to 600 strong, under the following officers:—"Sir Duncan Campbel, John Aylief, and the Laird of Lapness (Elphinstone), were Colonels; Major Alexander Campbel, the Laird of Barbreck, and a third, were Lieutenant-Colonels; James Henderson, John Fullarton, and Major John Campbell were Majors; and all inferior officers were at the Time nominate, and this Handful put in the best Order might be."

In good time the ships of war arrived in the harbour from Campbeltown. They were three in number, the largest carrying thirty-six guns, the second twelve, and the third six, while in addition they had a small vessel laden with corn, which they had captured upon the coast.

But whilst Argyll's forces were thus increased in numbers, as time passed their prospects of

success, whatever they might be, were greatly
reduced by the ceaseless quarrels and intrigues of
some of the Lowlanders. "The bickerings," says
Lord Macaulay, "which had begun in Holland, had
never been intermitted during the whole course of
the expedition; but at Tarbet they became more
violent than ever." There being but six hundred
Government troops in Argyllshire, and these in the
neighbourhood of Inveraray, it was the Earl's desire
to proceed there in the first instance, in order to
expel them from the shire, which might easily be
done, and raise more of his clansmen before passing
to the Lowlands, but Sir John Cochran and some
others of like mind were determined to proceed
direct to Ayrshire, where they expected large numbers of the people to join them for the support of
the Covenant. In their Highland allies they had
little faith, regarding them as "half-papists," who
had joined the enterprise simply for the sake of
the Earl. To decide matters a council of war was
held, and it was there resolved, contrary to the
will of Argyll, that an invasion should be forthwith made on the Lowlands. Accordingly, on the
29th of May, two days after his arrival on the
isthmus, the Earl "loosed from the Tarbet and
came into the town of Rosa in the isle of Boot,
where he took a night's provision for himself and
his men." The ultimate fate of this ill-starred
expedition is too well known to require lengthened
mention here. Some of the party had a successful

skirmish at Greenock, when they "tooke some meal
out of a girnull, and a pretty barque out of the
harbour, and returned to Rothesay.   While wee
were away, the Erle had caused burn the Castle,
because a house of his had been burnt in Cowall."

Evading the king's ships and forces, they effected
a landing, but while marching through Dumbartonshire for Glasgow, the little army was broken up
at Kilpatrick on the 18th June.   After crossing
the river Clyde, Argyll was taken prisoner at
Inchinnan, on the river Cart, and carried to Edinburgh, where he was beheaded twelve days there-
after.   Thus died the Earl of Argyll.   Shortly
afterwards, viz., on June 16th, an Act of the
Scottish Parliament was passed by which certain
offices, jurisdictions, &c., long possessed by the
house of Argyll, were "united, annexed, and incor-
porated to the Crown of this his (James II.)
Ancient Kingdome, to remaine inseparably ther-
with in all time Coming," viz., *inter alia,* the offices
of Justice General, Heritable Lieutenant, Chamberlain, Sheriff, and Coroner of " Argyll and Tarbert
Shires ;" and of constable of the castle of Tarbert,
and superior of the lands of Tarbert, &c.   In
indicating the necessity for this confiscation, the
Act states that the possession of so many offices
had raised the Campbells to too great power.   Of
short duration, however, was this deprivation of
offices and power, a complete restoration having
been effected by the Revolution of 1688, when the

last of the Stuarts was hurried from that throne
which he had made the abode of tyranny and
violence.

For many months after the landing of William
and Mary, and before their power was thoroughly
established, the state of the country continued very
unsettled.　In May, 1689, the Committee of
Estates having received notice that "some Irishes"
had landed in Kintyre, ordered four companies of
Lord Bargany's regiment, two companies of the
Earl of Glencairn's regiment, and two of Lord
Blantyre's regiment to march to Largs or other
convenient port on the west coast, and there take
ship for Tarbert, where they were to unite with
some companies, or the whole of the Earl of
Argyll's regiment.　In addition to this force, Sir
Duncan Campbell, of Auchinbreck, Lieutenant-
Colonel of the latter regiment, was further em-
powered to call together, if necessary, "all the
fencible men in the continent of the shyres of
Argyll and Tarbert, and to keep them in armes for
defence of the countrie."　That the "Irishes" were
not to be lightly dealt with is apparent from the
tenor of Auchinbreck's orders, he being strictly
enjoined to "persew, kill, and dissipate any per-
sones who shall appear in oppositione to the
Government."

On this occasion the natives of Kintyre and that
neighbourhood, in accordance with their wonted

enmity to the Campbells, also rose in arms, but
were subdued after a few skirmishes.

At the period referred to, the chief support of
James came from his co-religionists in Ireland,
large numbers of Roman Catholic soldiers having
been enlisted by Tyrconnel. On June 27th of this
same year we find Viscount Dundee, commander
of the forces that still adhered to James in Scotland,
writing to Lord Melfort, and appealing to him to
send over some reinforcements from that country.
After requesting that from 5000 to 6000 troops,
including 600 or 800 horse, might be landed at
Inverlochy, his letter proceeds thus:—"So soon as
the boats return, let them ferry over as many more
foot as they think fit to the Point of Kintyre,
which will soon be done. . . . . I should
march towards Kintyre, and meet at the neck of
Tarbitt the foot, and so march to raise the country,
and then towards the Passes of Forth to meet the
king." But the king he never met. Whether or
not Irish troops were sent to Kintyre cannot be
gathered. However that may be, Dundee's proposed march to Tarbert never occurred, the fatal
battle of Kiliecrankie having been fought, and
Clavers sent to meet that Judge he erstwhile
defied, ere an opportunity presented itself.

With the succeeding efforts in 1715 and 1745,
in the same direction, and in favour of the Pre-
tender and Prince Charlie, the history of Tarbert

is but lightly touched, the lairds and people of the
village and its neighbourhood having espoused the
Hanoverian cause. One incident, however, regarding the '45 may here be referred to. On this
occasion it was the intention of Macdonald of
Largie to join Prince Charlie, but he was hindered
in a manner which is variously stated. Cuthbert
Bede gives the following version on the authority
of the late Laird of Largie:—"In the 'Forty-five'
the then Laird of Largie was for going out. He
was to join with other lairds in taking ship at
Tarbert. The minister of Kilcalmonell invited him
to spend the night at the manse on his way to
Tarbert, and by the over-exercise of hospitality
contrived that Largie should be late in getting up
the next morning. And so it happened that when
Largie arrived at Tarbert with his contingent the
fleet had sailed. Thus was the property of Largie
saved in '45. Afterwards Largie went to Paris and
gave great entertainments to the Prince, whereby
he got so much into debt as to be obliged to sell a
portion of his estates." From another source he
received this second version of the story:—"In the
'Forty-five' the proprietors of Kintyre raised their
men against Prince Charlie, but Macdonald of
Largie declared for the Prince. Upon this the
Laird of Tarbert sent him word that if he intended
to join the Prince, he would meet him on his way
in passing, and that they would have a hot day of
it, and that few Macdonald's should remain to join

any party.   On this the Laird of Largie thought fit
to change his mind, so he sent his men with the
rest of the men of Kintyre " to Inveraray.

CHAPTER VII.

LAIRDS OF TARBERT—THE M'ALISTERS AND
CAMPBELLS.

A S far back as the sixteenth century may be
traced the connection with the village of
the old M'Alisters of Tarbert, the former proprietors, to the last of whom reference has been
made in the closing sentence of the preceding
chapter.

According to Mackenzie's "History of the
Macdonalds," the M'Alisters claim their descent
from Alexander, eldest son of Angus Mor, Lord of
the Isles, but their real descent seems to have been
from Alexander, second son of Donald of the Isles,
and younger brother of Angus Mor.

In the "Register of the Privy Seal" for the
year 1515 appears the name of "Angus Vic Ean

Dubh." This Angus, who was chief of the M'Alisters and Laird of Loup (an estate in Kintyre ten miles from Tarbert), had three sons, the second of whom, Donald, founded the Tarbert branch of the clan, and was constable of the castle, an office which became hereditary with them, and which they continued to hold for centuries as the vassals of the house of Argyll.

Next to the M'Alisters of Loup this branch would seem to have been the most important. From references existing in several authorities to the successors of Donald, we find the following mentioned as subsequent lairds. According to the " Origines Parochiales," the possessor of the estates in the year 1580 was Charles M'Alister. From the " Register of the Privy Council " we learn that in 1602 Archibald M'Alister, who was concerned in some raids into Bute, was then the heir apparent to the Tarbert estates. In the years 1667 and 1678 Ronald was laird, and at these dates he was Commissioner of Supply for the shire of Argyll. The next to whom reference is made is a second Archibald. He was in possession in 1685, and in his favour an act, for the institution of fairs in the village, was passed by the Scottish Parliament in the year 1705. Charles, the successor of the above, died in the year 1741, and was buried in the churchyard of Tarbert. On a marble tablet set in the wall surrounding the tomb may be read the following inscription to his memory, and to that of his wife, who was a daughter of Walter Campbell of Skipness:—

" S. M.
CAROLI M'ALISTER
DE TARBERT,
QUI OBIIT 3ᵁˢ· AP., 1741,
AETAT.
ANNA CAMPBELL
FILIA GUALTERI CAMPBELL
DE SKIPNESS
TUM EJUS CONJUX
HOC MONUMENTUM
POSUIT."

Archibald, who succeeded to the estate, was the last of the line to inherit them, and with the severance of his connection, bonds were cut which had for centuries united the family with Tarbert and its fortune.

In military affairs of imperial interest the M'Alisters would appear to have been usually found on the side favoured by their superiors, the Argylls. Like other clans, however, in the days when might was right, they had their own feuds and skirmishes with their neighbours. Sallying from the castle and holding it as a base of operations and a place of safe retreat, they were particularly well situated either for holding their own or for making forays by sea or by land upon the adjacent territories.

On one occasion they were called upon to repel an invasion of the M'Ivers. A branch of this clan having settled at Lochgilp, and built a sort of

small fort on the west side of it, made many raids
on their southern neighbours. As the result of
two encounters, however, they were eventually
almost exterminated. The first of these occurred
with the M'Neils near the mouth of West Loch
Tarbert, and probably in the vicinity of Lergna-
hunsion; the second was the occasion referred to
above, in which they were seriously defeated
by the M'Alisters of Tarbert on the shores of
Lochfyne.

A favourite scene for the forays of the Knapdale
and Kintyre men was Arran, and from the
" Register of the Privy Council " it appears that
in connection with these, complaints by the proprietors of that picturesque island were frequently
made to the Government. In the raid into Bute
in 1602, spoken of formerly, Archibald M'Alister,
younger of Tarbert, was accompanied by Campbell
of Auchinbreck, Colin Campbell, apparent of Kilberry, M'Neil of Taynish, &c., with a following of
about 1200 men.

During the confiscation of Argyll, and while the
followers of Athole were plundering the Campbells
in all directions to their hearts' content, M'Alister
also seized the opportunity which presented of
enriching himself by making frequent raids on the
territory of his former feudal superiors. Issuing
from the shelter of the castle, Innellan and Colintraive on the one hand, and Inveraray on the other
were laid under contribution.

On one occasion, during June and July, 1685, we learn from " The Depredations committed on the Clan Campbell in 1685 and 1686," that articles of a most miscellaneous character, valued at £773 6s 8d Scots, were " lifted " from " Neil Campbell of Ellengreig" and his tenants at Colintraive and its neighbourhood by " Donald M'Ilvorie (M'Gilvray) in Tarbert, tennent to Archibald M'Alister of Tarbert, and then his follower and servant," M'Eachern, M'Iffie (M'Phee), who were also "in Tarbert's companie," and their accomplices. A complete list of the articles, stock, &c., removed is given, and the statement is interesting as giving an idea of the character of conveniences, and the sources of wealth at that date. Everything that they could lay their hands on seems to have been included in their booty—horses, cows, sheep, geese, money, a ferry-boat (Colintraive), a gray plaid, a dirk, plough irons, hides, an anchor tow (rope), herring nets, meal, an axe, brewing graith, barrels empty and full, tables, chests, doors, a pot and crook, a brass pan, a standing bed, and other household plenishings.

Continuing their excursion, and visiting the Captain of Dunoon's tenants at Innellan, they added to their plunder by killing "nyne great coues," valued at £140 Scots, and took possession, further, of cloth and other articles to the value of £50. From Pennymoir, from Inveraray, and from Auchinshellich, considerable contributions of a miscellaneous character were also secured during these same months. Such were the little diversions of the Highlanders of the seventeenth century.

As to the disastrous effect of such raids on the country at large, they were only too well borne home to the Governments of these days, and with a view to fostering the arts of peace, establishing friendly intercourse, and furthering civilisation, many means were had recourse to from time to time. Among these was the establishment of fairs and markets in convenient localities. As far back as the year 1705 Tarbert was fixed upon for this purpose, as is formerly mentioned incidentally, and in September of that year an Act of the Scottish Parliament was passed instituting the same. The Act, among the last passed by the Parliament of Scotland, is somewhat interesting, and may be quoted in full. It is as follows:—

"ACT IN FAVORS OF ARCHBALD MACKALESTER OF TARBET
FOR FOUR YEARLY FAIRS AND A WEEKLY MERCAT
AT THE TOUN OF EAST TARBET.

Our Sovereign Lady and Estates of Parliament considering that fairs and mercats in convenient places tend much to the good and advantage of the Inhabitants thereof and of Her Majesties other Leidges dwelling near thereto, and that it is very fit for these ends to authorize four yearly fairs and a weekly mercat at the Toun of East Tarbet, in the shire of Argyll, belonging to Archbald Mackalester of Tarbet, Do therefore by thir presents Appoint four fairs to be kept and holden yearly in all time comeing, One thereof to begin upon the tenth day of May, Another to begin on the sixteenth day of July, Another to begin upon the nineteenth day of August,

And the other to begin upon the sixteenth day of October, and each of them to continue two dayes, And a weekly mercat to be holden in all time comeing every Tuesday at the said Toun of East Tarbet. And have Given and Granted and hereby Give and Grant to the said Archbald Mackalester his heirs and successors the right and priviledge of keeping the said yearly fairs and weekly mercats for all kinds of merchandice with all the tolls customes and casualities thereof and all other liberties priviledges and immunities and advantages used and wont to belong to any haveing the priviledge of keeping fairs and mercats within this Kingdom."

It will be observed that none of the above dates corresponds with that on which the yearly fair has been for long held, viz., the last Thursday in July, nor yet with the dates of either of the other three yearly markets recently established.

According to the "Statistical Account of Scotland," published towards the end of last century, the Macalisters of Tarbert had been "by far the most considerable family in South Knapdale." Although descended from the Macdonalds, all their lands were held on feu charters granted by the Argylls. In their more prosperous days almost all the lands for some miles around Tarbert were in their possession, while northwards their territory extended along the coasts of Lochfyne and Lochgilp, to the very extremity of South Knapdale parish.

Evil days, however, overtook the family. From some cause or other (according to one story, from the amount of his wine merchant's bills), Archibald M'Alister became very poor ; his lands were heavily mortgaged, and by degrees passed into other hands, so that some years before the middle of the last century, the ancient stock ceased to be the possessors of a single acre. Dael and Craiglass became the property of Mr Macarthur Stewart, of Milton, and the other lands north of Inverneil fell to Mr Peter Dow Campbell, of Kildusclan (a title taken from the name of a small chapel on the shore of Lochgilp). Four farms constituting the Erin's estate became possessed by Mr Macfarlane, of Muckroy; three more were formed into the estate of Kintarbert, and became the property of Campbell of Kintarbert, from whom the late proprietrix, Miss M'Neil-Campbell, was descended; while the remainder of the original estate, with the mansion house which was situated at Barmore, just below the position occupied by the present residence, was purchased in 1746 by Archibald Campbell of Stonefield, great-great-grandfather of the present estemable Laird.

" Sic transit gloria mundi."

By this time Tarbert Castle had fallen seriously into disrepair, and this fact, together with others that shall appear, formed the subject of an important and unique lawsuit which the Duke of Argyll instituted against the last M'Alister laird, or rather against his creditors, in the year 1762, and which may be here referred to.

While the M'Alisters were yet in prosperous circumstances, they had built for themselves the mansion-house at Barmore indicated above, and the castle being no longer required to serve its original purpose of a fort, its condition was neglected, contrary to the stipulations of the old charter. In feudal times, as is well known, the conditions on which lands, castles, &c., were held by a vassal were mainly those of service, the grant being made by the Superior and confirmed by the Sovereign. In the case of the Barony of Skipness and the keeping of its castle for example, the Earl of Argyll in 1511 conferred them on one of his sons upon the following conditions, viz., " furnishing two galleys, one of sixteen and one of fourteen oars, for the Earl's service when required, and paying yearly at the Castle of Skippinych twenty-four bolls meal, twenty-four bolls bear, and thirty-seven stones of cheese." The following excerpt from the feu-charter, which contains the points on which the action was based, is interesting, as showing to some extent the conditions on which the Tarbert estate was held, while the result of the suit (so far as concluded) in connection with some of the points raised, illustrates the transition state of the law at this period when a tithe of feudalism still existed. The charter, the original of which is in Latin, among other things stipulated that the vassal should provide—

" A boat of six oars in time of peace and war, which they shall be bound to equip properly with arms and all necessaries, along with six rowers and a steersman for the service of our S.D.N. . . lord the king, and us and our heirs and descendants for transporting us and our aforesaids from Tarbert to Strondour, Silvercraigs, and Lochgear ; and likewise to any part of Cowal between the promontory of Aird and the Strait of Ottar, at the cost and expense of the said Archd. M'Alister and his heirs, as often as required.   And likewise the said Archibald M'Alister .and his aforesaids shall be bound faithfully, steadfastly, and securely to watch, ward, and defend the said castle and fortalice for the use and service of us and our aforesaids from the attacks of our enemies and foes, and to receive and guard prisoners in the said castle at the expense of us and our aforesaids, whenever they receive a command from us or our aforesaids, or our deputies from time to time.   And that they will be faithful and obedient unto us and our aforesaids in all other things incumbent on the office of keeper of the said castle, as the other captains and keepers of our other castles and houses within the shire of Argyll shall be bound and are wont to do.   And likewise to preserve and maintain the said castle of Tarbert wind and water tight in all time coming at the cost and expense of the said Archibald M'Alister and his aforesaids, and to receive and entertain us and our aforesaids, whenever we come to the said castle, in the same manner as the other keepers of our castles are wont to do."

In prosecuting his suit before the Lords of Session, Argyll admitted that the obligation contained in the charter to keep and defend the castle for the use of the Superior could not now be lawfully enacted, while he also agreed to pass from the clause obliging the vassal to support the fabric and maintain it wind and water tight for the reception and entertainment of the Superior gratis, provided the vassal became bound to uphold the mansion house lately built on the feu in the same manner and for the same lawful purpose.   The clause referring to the boat and rowers he also insisted on, and contended that these several prestations should be performed and declared real burdens on the estate.

For the creditors it was objected that the obligations of keeping up a house and a boat for receiving and entertaining the Superior, and for transporting him from one place to another, fell under an Act of George I., which discharges all personal services and attendance of vassals on their Superior, and ordains the same to be converted into an annual value in money.

In reply, it was contended for the pursuer that the Legislature did not mean to abolish all personal obligations in charters, but only such as formerly gave Superiors an opportunity of convocating their vassals. By the preamble of the Statute, all service, with the exception of personal attendance, shooting, hunting, watching, and warding, were reserved, their purpose being entirely innocent.

The Lords, in giving judgement, found as follows:

"That the pursuer's vassal in the Estate of Tarbert is bound upon his own proper charges and expenses to keep and uphold a boat of six oars, and to provide the same with six rowers and a steersman and all things necessary for the use of the Superior and his family, in terms of the former feu charters thereof : and also to keep the mansion house now built upon said estate wind and water tight: and find that the prestations are not personal services, and do not fall under the statute of George I. founded on, but that the future feu rights of said estate ought to be burdened therewith, and to contain a reddendo in these terms ; and remit to the Lord

Ordinary to proceed accordingly. But with respect to that part of the reddendo of the former charters whereby the vassal is bound to receive and entertain the Superior and his heirs, gratis, in his Castle of Tarbert in the same way as the other Keepers of the Pursuer's Castles are bound to do, they remit to the Lord Ordinary to hear parties further, and do therein as he shall see cause."

This decision was considered of much importance, and it became a precedent for future actions of a similar nature.

Archibald Campbell of Stonefield, who purchased in 1746 the larger part of M'Alister's estate, and whose descendants continue still in possession, was a cadet of the house of Lochnell. By the male line the family is descended from John Gorm, second son of Colin, third Earl of Argyll, while by the female side they trace their descent from the Breadalbane stock through Sir John Campbell of Glenorchy, father of the first Earl of that ilk. The title of Stonefield is derived from the name of an estate which they formerly possessed on the picturesque shores of Loch Etive, and under the shadow of Ben Cruachan. It is now known by its Gaelic name of Auchnacloich.

After selling their estates in this region, as well as some possessions in the island of Lismore, the Stonefields became connected with the Tarbert district as early as the year 1716 or 1717, by the purchase from the Campbells of Blythswood of a portion of their present estate situated to the south and west of Bardaravine burn. At this period the family were also possessed of estates in the parish of Kilmaronock, in the north of Dumbartonshire, while about the same time as they purchased the above land in the vicinity of Tarbert they became proprietors of the estate of Strathleven (then called Stonefield), situated in the neighbourhood of the town of Dumbarton.

For many years Sheriff-depute of Argyll and Bute, Archibald Campbell would seem to have been a gentleman of much ability, determination, and resolution. He did much to improve the estate, and by his energy in enclosing it, and draining and planting extensively, increased its value very considerably. About this time important and very necessary efforts were made to improve the roads throughout Argyllshire, and in connection with those in the neighbourhood of Tarbert, Stonefield exerted himself in no light degree. This is well illustrated by an incident relating to the making of the road between Ardrishaig and Tarbert, which is given in the "New Statistical Account":—

" The Sliabh Ghaoil road, which was so useful before the introduction of steam, and conferred such a boon on the country generally, and on Kintyre particularly, was obtained through the instrumentality of Sheriff Campbell, one of the ancestors of the present family of Stonefield. The line was surveyed by an English engineer. It is said that he attempted to travel over the ground, but the rocks were so precipitous, the ferns so gigantic, the Englishman so unwieldly, and so unaccustomed to travel such rough grounds, that, after much tumbling and scrambling, he was obliged to betake himself to his boat, and finish his survey by rowing along the shore. On arriving at Barmore House, the residence of Sheriff Campbell, he remarked to the Sheriff that it was a hopeless thing to attempt opening a road along the projected line ; that it was an undertaking fit for the Empress Catherine of Russia, and not fit for private individuals. The Sheriff ordered his clerk or treasurer to pay the English surveyor for his trouble, and with that determination and resolution which so much characterised that gentleman, the Sheriff set about the mighty task of opening the Sliabh Ghaoil road, and persevered till it was finished. . . . .

Before the opening of this road, the district of Kintyre was quite insulated from the rest of Argyleshire. The only path by which any communication between the two places could be maintained was almost quite impassable. It ran along hills and dales which were intersected by water courses without any bridges, In summer the waters were fordable, but in winter the attempt to cross them was both difficult and dangerous."

In carrying out this costly but useful undertaking, the Sheriff was ably assisted by His Grace the Duke of Argyll, and the gentlemen of the shire in general, who contributed liberally towards its accomplishment.

On the death of Archibald Campbell, which occurred in the year 1777, he was buried at Arrivore, six miles from Tarbert, where was another residence of the family. He was succeeded in the estates by his son John, judicially styled Lord Stonefield. A daughter, Elizabeth, married John Campbell of Carwhin, and became the mother of the fourth earl and first marquis of Breadalbane.

Lord Stonefield was an eminent judge. "Admitted advocate in 1748, he was elevated to the bench of the Court of Session in 1762. In 1787 he succeeded Lord Gardenstone as a lord of justiciary, which appointment, however, he resigned in 1792, retaining his seat in the Court of Session till his death, 19th June, 1801, having been thirty-nine years a judge of the supreme court. By his wife, Lady Grace Stuart, daughter of James, second Earl of Bute, and sister of the Prime Minister, John, third earl, Lord Stonefield had seven sons, all of whom predeceased him." Colin, his eldest son, was Colonel of the Dumbarton Fencibles, which regiment he was instrumental in raising in the year 1794. After serving in Ireland during the rebellion, they returned to Scotland in 1802, and were reduced the same year. The second son, Lieutenant-Colonel John Campbell, was the hero of Mangalore, the soldier whose memorable defence of that town from May, 1783, to January of the following year, first arrested the victorious career of Tippoo Sultan. Born in 1753, this illustrious soldier entered the army in the eighteenth year of his age. He served successively in the 57th regiment, the 7th foot (with the latter in Canada, where he was taken prisoner), the 71st, and the 74th. By this time he had reached the rank of Major. In 1781 he exchanged into the 100th regiment, and with this corps he served with distinction in the East Indies against the troops of Hyder Ali, during which

HIGHLAND COTTAGES.

Bennett & Thomson,   Lithographers

TARBERT CASTLE

TARBERT FROM THE EAST.

BENNETT & THOMSON,

BENNETT & THOMSON,

HERRING SKIFFS.

Lithographers

period he was appointed to the majority of the
42nd. Wounded in an engagement with Tippoo
Sultan, he refused to quit the field till the enemy
was defeated. He was afterwards engaged in the
siege of Annantpore, which he reduced and took
from the enemy. In May, 1783, he was appointed
to the provisional command of the army in the
Bidnure country, and soon found himself called
upon to defend the important fortress of Mangalore
against the prodigious force of Tippoo Sultan.
Tippoo's force was estimated at 140,000 men, with
a hundred pieces of artillery, and the defence of
the town by Major Campbell, with a garrison
numbering only 1883, of whom but two or three
hundred were British soldiers, " is justly accounted
one of the most remarkable achievements that ever
signalized the British arms in India." For two and
a half months this little garrison resisted all the
efforts of Tippoo. Breach after breach was made,
which the besiegers attempted to storm, but they
were invariably driven back at the bayonet's point.
For a brief period a cessation of hostilities took
place, and then for a time the siege was turned into
a blockade. Twice did Colonel M·Leod appear off
the port, with ships filled with troops; but instead
of landing them and attacking Tippoo in his camp,
he made agreements with that barbarian for per-
mission for the garrison to procure supplies, which
agreements Tippoo carried out by ordering all
persons to sell them nothing but damaged and

putrid stores. The bravery and resolution displayed by Major Campbell were so much admired by Tippoo that he expressed a wish to see him. The Major, accompanied by several of his officers, accordingly waited upon him, when "he presented to each of them a handsome shawl; and after their return to the fort, he sent Major Campbell an additional present of a very fine horse, which the famishing garrison afterwards killed and ate." After sustaining a siege of eight months, during which they were reduced to the greatest extremities by disease and famine, the garrison at length capitulated on the 24th January, 1784, on the understanding that they were to march out with all the honours of war. Accordingly they evacuated the fort on the 30th, and embarked for Tillicherry, one of the British settlements, on the coast of Malabar. Major Campbell now attained the rank of Lieutenant-Colonel; but the fatigue which he endured during the siege had undermined his constitution, and in the following month he was obliged by ill health to quit the army and retire to Bombay, where he died on the 23rd of March, in the 31st year of his age. To his memory a monument was erected in the church at Bombay, by order of the East India Company.

Lord Stonefield having been predeceased by all his sons, he was succeeded in the estates by his grandson, John, eldest son of Colonel Colin Campbell. By him Stonefield house, the present residence at Barmore, was erected, and many important improvements effected on the estate. He died on March 18th, 1857, and was buried at the new tomb situated half-a-mile further north than the house. By his wife, who was a daughter of Sir James Colquhoun, Bart. of Luss, he left two sons, Colin George Campbell, the present laird, and James Colquhoun Campbell, D.D., Lord Bishop of Bangor. The former was for many years Convener of the County of Argyll. The Bishop, having graduated in honours at Trinity College, Cambridge, was successively appointed rector of Merthyr Tydvil, and Archdeacon of Llandaff, and was nominated by Lord Derby to the See of Bangor in April, 1859.

CHAPTER VIII.

TARBERT IN RECENT TIMES.

ALTHOUGH till within the last fifty years Tarbert could not boast of a population of more than 750 inhabitants, its importance as a centre of trade and communication was, as has been already shown, always very considerable. In the year 1809, we learn that a memorial was presented to the Parliamentary Commissioners, in which it was stated that the village of Tarbert was "one of the most considerable places in the West Highlands, on account of the excellence of its harbour and the peculiar advantages of its locality. It is the centre of communication between the numerous sea lochs that indent the coast of this part of the country, and offers great facilities of transit between the districts on the east and west." The object of this memorial was to endeavour to induce Government to undertake the renewal of the land breast originally constructed by the proprietor, and the enlargement of the quay.

In answer to the memorialists, the Commissioners "agreed to the enlargement of the quay, the renewing of the land breast which had become ruinous, and the improvement of the approaches to the harbour by the removal of some rocks obstructing the entrance."

Just about this date the more modern village sprang into existence. Houses now began to be built on what has since been the front or main street, the older ones having been situated further inland, and on the hillsides. The maintenance of the breast wall to stay the winter tides has on this account also become absolutely indispensable, yet even now the lower flats of many of the houses are occasionally invaded by the unwelcome visitor. After a lapse of eighty years, however, these structures continue in good repair, and have proved a boon of no ordinary character to the villagers.

To the convenient situation of the harbour and its excellence as an anchorage is doubtless due the pre-eminence which Tarbert holds as the centre of the Lochfyne herring fishery. Within its kindly shelter have been reared many generations of hardy fishermen, who by their perseverance, diligence, and devotion to the occupation of their forefathers, and by their readiness to adopt those methods which have proved most remunerative, have demonstrated how success may be obtained even in a calling which is notoriously one of the most fickle and uncertain.

East Loch Tarbert, which constitutes the harbour, is an arm of Lochfyne one mile in length and three furlongs in breadth at its widest part, with an island about its centre dividing the harbour into an inner and an outer portion. While the island serves to render the inner bay thoroughly secure, the passage on either hand is so narrow that to see for the first time a steamer threading its way in either direction is to make one almost conclude that she is running to certain destruction.

Along the sides of this land-locked basin the great bulk of the houses constituting the village are situated. Forming a short street behind is the older part of the village proper, which until lately consisted almost entirely of small and very unpretentious thatched houses, more picturesque than inviting. This old street, however, boasts of having been one of the first paved streets in the kingdom. In it stands also an old modest thatched cottage, in which it is said justice used to be dispensed in those days when Tarbert was yet the headquarters of a Sheriff. Whether it is the original court-house or not, the existing house—which is still occupied as a dwelling, and was at one time used as an inn—stands, it would seem, on the original site. By means of an underground vault it communicates with an adjoining house. It is probable the purpose of this vault was not as a place of safety, as might be inferred, but to serve the ends of illicit distilling, which is said to have been extensively carried on within it. The usual difficulty with regard to the smoke is understood to have been overcome by introducing it into the chimney of the court-house. In connection with the vault the following story is told:—A good many years ago a son of Afric's soil, on the evening of the July Fair, was lodging in the house which has been referred to as adjoining the old court-house. Throughout the evening dancing was indulged in, the bottle circulated freely, and he of the sable countenance shared in the general merriment. As the night wore on, the enthusiasm of the latter and the vigour of his movements increased with the growing excitement and the cumulative influence of the Highlanders' strong water. A Scotch reel was in progress. Not to be outdone by the efforts of his Celtic fellow-dancers, Sambo *reeled* and *set* with renewed energy, till all on a sudden, as he uttered a mighty "hooch," the flooring gave way, and down he plunged into the vault beneath. Being persuaded that the end of the world had come, and that the earth had just opened its mouth quietly to receive him, it is not to be wondered at that his "hooch" very quickly degenerated into a yell of despair, as he felt himself descend into the darkness.

In addition to the front street and back street, there exist on all sides numerous cottages, which have been lately erected both for the accommodation of the increasing population and for the convenience of summer visitors.

Situated as the village is on the isthmus which connects Kintyre with the lands of Knapdale, it encroaches on both districts, the larger half being in Kintyre. Its parochial affairs are for the same reason controlled by the authorities of two parishes, the Kintyre portion being in the united parishes of Kilcalmonell and Kilberry, and the Knapdale portion in that of South Knapdale.

The general appearance of the village is very pleasing. You have arrived, we shall say, some fine day by the good ship "Columba," which calls at the outer pier, constructed at a distance of rather less than a mile from the centre of the village by the present laird in the year 1866. Choosing either to drive or walk, you pass on your left hand a very handsome and commodious hotel, recently erected. Beyond it, and lining the road as it skirts the water, are about half-a-dozen tastefully built villas, which have sprung up within the last four or five years. Now you come in sight of the hoary ruin, the old guardian of the village, which looks down from its craggy height, unmoved, on the changes which time has wrought around. Under its shadow a second group of neat cottages with their gardens has been erected, and proceeding a little further a turn in the road brings you in sight of the greater portion of the village, snugly nestling under the shelter of its hills. Just before

entering the village the old pier is passed, at which
the *goods* steamers call, and where in days gone
by so many busy scenes were witnessed in connection with the landing, curing, and shipping of
herring.

With an extensive country district to provide for
besides the village population of about 1850 souls,
the demand for the conveniences of civilization is
met not inefficiently. Two churches, an Established
one crowning an eminence to the west of the village
—a veritable Mount Zion—and a Free, modestly
hiding itself behind the main street, provide for the
spiritual edification of the people. The former is
quite an imposing new structure, reflecting credit
on the parishioners, and occupies a site which makes
it a most prominent feature in the landscape.

Although, as we have seen, a chapel existed in
pre-reformation times in connection with the castle,
and although there is also reason to suppose that a
chapel at one time existed at Glenakil, Tarbert for
long was dependent on the occasional ministrations
of the Parish ministers, who resided, one at Clachan
and the other at Achoish. The old church, which
has just been replaced, was built in the year 1775,
when "a mission was established by the committee
for the management of the Royal Bounty, and a
missionary appointed to preach there every Sab-
bath." Till about twenty years ago it continued a
mission station, but at this date it was raised to the
position of a *Quoad Sacra* parish, the sum of a

thousand pounds sterling having been subscribed for that purpose.

Steps have lately been taken by the Free Church community with a view to following up the example of their Established brethren, and erecting a handsome and commodious structure to replace the present church, which was built under difficulties at the Disruption, and which has well served its day and generation.

As necessary adjuncts to the churches, both are provided with very creditable manses, that of the Free Church looking down on the village from the north, and that of the Established erected on the isthmus close by the church.

On a cheerful and healthy situation to the rear of the village is the school-house, where the youthful intellects are duly moulded in conformity with the most approved Government pattern.

Contiguous with the school-house is the residence of the head master, the whole building forming a delightfully irregular construction after no particular style of architecture.

Within the last dozen years very great improvements have been made in the houses generally. Shops of a character much superior to the run of villages of a like size exist in abundance, evidencing considerable enterprise on the part of the inhabitants, and an abundant faith in plenteous harvests being yet gathered from the sea.

As indicating a certain amount of prosperty, and the development of habits of thrift, it is gratifying to observe the large number of cottages which have been erected within recent years by the fishermen. At least a score of comfortable and well built houses of from four to eight apartments, each with its garden attached, have sprung up within the last fifteen years in the outskirts of the village, all of which are partially occupied by the owners, and many let to summer visitors. These, together with a few larger and more pretentious villas, give to the place a much more *coast-like* appearance than formerly, and add not a little to its attractions as a summer resort.

Regarding hotel accommodation, a very necessary feature in the equipment of a coast village, it is ample. The principal hotel is the "Tarbert," and here, under the genial and homely management of Mrs M'Lean, who has been so long at the head of it, the wayfarer finds himself as comfortable and well tended as it is possible to be away from his "ain fireside."

A branch of the Union Bank looks after the safe keeping of the surplus cash, and affords the necessary facilities for the transaction of business.

About fourteen years ago there was founded in the village a lodge of the Independent Order of Good Templars, which since its formation has done much good service, more particularly among the fishermen. For convenience of meeting, the mem-

bers banded themselves together and erected a hall
in 1872, capable of holding about 400 people. Till
this date the village was entirely dependent on
the school-house for a place of meeting. Since then
this hall has been generously given free of charge
by the Templars, when required for any purpose
purely intended to benefit the village, and it has
consequently been of much value to the community.

The Volunteer movement which originated in
1859 found early adherents among the young men
of Tarbert. Previous to the formation of a battery
in the village, the Tarbert enthusiasts exhibited
their loyalty and their love of arms by forming a
section in connection with the now defunct Dunmore Corps, or 4th A.A.V., raised by the late Major
Campbell of Dunmore. In 1866 a local battery,
the 11th A.A.V., having as a nucleus the older
Volunteers, was formed under the command of C.
G. Campbell, Esq., of Stonefield; Messrs Hugh
M'Lean and James E. M'Larty acting as lieutenants. After a few years the late John Campbell, younger of Stonefield, became captain in room
of his father, who resigned, and he continued to
hold the position till his untimely death in the
beginning of 1885.

After a service of twenty-five years in the ranks,
a few of the original members, still active and
zealous, remain connected with the Corps, and may
well be considered veterans among the thousands
who have joined throughout the land, and have

fitted themselves to stand up for Queen and Country, since the institution of the Volunteer movement.

With a strength of sixty-three, the greater number of whom are active young fishermen, thoroughly fitted for the duties of gunners, the Battery continues under its present officers in a thoroughly efficient state, providing healthful recreation and instruction for the youth of the village, and contributing its little quota to the security of the State.

A great institution of the village, and one full of interest to the lads and lasses, the boys and girls of all the surrounding district, is Tarbert Fair, which is held on the last Thursday of July. It is the high day of the year. Every one is dressed in holiday attire, and everyone gives himself or herself up to simple social enjoyment.

The ostensible reason for the fair is the sale of horses and wool; yet, although a pretty large business is done in both, it fails to account for the enormous crowds that flock to the village on such occasions. By road and by steamer they come, walking, driving, sailing. The reason is in most cases of a sociable rather than of a commercial nature. Here, as at a convenient centre, every one meets his relatives, " from the brother of his blood to his cousin forty times removed ; " the lads and lasses of Tarbert, Campbeltown, and the country districts of Kintyre mingle with those from Arran, Bute

Cowal, Lochgilphead, Kilmartin, Knapdale, and Kilberry, and many are the hand shakings and warm the greetings as friend meets with friend once again, these occasions being in many instances the only ones on which they have an opportunity of associating with one another throughout the year. Every lassie has a variety of laddies, and every Jocky has his Jenny on that day, and well does Jocky's pocket know it before the day has expired. Fairings, in the shape of "sweeties," are innumerable, and no acquaintance of the other sex does he meet but she must be treated, and her already swollen handbag still further expanded with those special tokens of esteem and friendship. To such an extent is this species of gallantry carried that some of the more particularly attractive young ladies find it necessary to purchase large message baskets in order to carry home their spoils. With such a wealth of confectionery such young ladies find themselves in a position to be particularly liberal to their less fortunate friends and acquaintances during the next year.

For months the boys and girls have been saving up every penny so that they may be able to avail themselves of the varied attractions which appeal so stronly to the juvenile eye and ear. The shooting stands and saloons, the toy stalls, the shows, the circus, the swings, and the merry-go-rounds, all must be patronised and enjoyed over and over again.

'Tis a busy day at Tarbert, and in fine weather the bargaining of the dealers, the laughing and chattering of the good-natured crowd as it moves slowly along, the music of the shows, with their gaudy exteriors, the tramping and rushing of horses through the crowd, and the many little incidents that are continually occurring in such circumstances all conspire to produce a scene of not a little gaiety and excitement. As evening closes, and the steamers take their departure, the crowd is lessened considerably, and the later hours, when the village is all ablaze with the lights of the numerous stalls, &c., are left to be enjoyed by the villagers and dwellers in the more immediate neighbourhood.

Besides this Fair three other markets have been lately held each year, but their importance is slight in comparison.

CHAPTER IX.

TRAWLERS AND TRAWLING.

NOTWITHSTANDING a considerable country trade and extensive shipments of wood, sheep, cattle, and wool, the staple of Tarbert's industry and the chief source of its prosperity is, as is well known wherever a Lochfyne herring is enjoyed, the herring fishery. Far and near the herring of Lochfyne are known as the finest and most delicate of their kind, and when fished in season, and cooked well, and in a perfectly fresh state, furnish forth a dish fit to gratify the palate of a prince.

The village has not inaptly been called the capital of herringdom. That it is devoted to fishing is on every hand very apparent. The rich brown nets, of beautiful workmanship, hanging from poles erected along the shores of the bay, waving gently their long folds in the breeze; the numerous plentifully-scaled fishing boats, of various forms and sizes, that dot the waters of the harbour, or line the inner breastwork; the fleet of smart-looking screw steamers which, holding the harbour as their headquarters, issue forth in the evening in quest of the fruits of the night's fishing; and the groups of stalwart fresh-coloured men, in their blue flannel and plaiding suits, long sea-boots, and mayhap a picturesque sou'-wester, which one meets every here and there, it may be idly discussing politics or the last night's catch while they await the time to start for the fishing-ground, or it may be busily engaged in mending nets (an ever recurrent and troublesome duty), all proclaim the community to be zealous worshippers of Neptune, and earnest seekers after the treasures of the briny deep.

The fishermen of Tarbert are thoroughgoing trawlers, so much so, indeed, that scarcely a native drift-net boat issues from the bay. At the time, some twenty years ago, when, by a short-sighted and easily misled Government, free trade in fishing was prohibited and trawling declared illegal, nowhere was the law more frequently broken than here, in spite of frequent imprisonments and numerous confiscations of boats and nets, and many were the rows and stirring the times when gunboats and special police endeavoured in vain to repress the system. That such attempts at limiting the method of fishing constituted a moral, commercial, and scientific mistake was abundantly

evidenced by the declarations of successive Royal
Commissions, and the following dialogue, taken
from Black's " Princess of Thule," illustrates not
unfairly some of its consequences, and the prejudicial effect it had on the manners and morals
of men who believed themselves to be treated
unjustly and harshly, and who were thus tempted
to break the law. Mackenzie, the " King of Borva,"
is represented as speaking thus :—

" I can say for them, Mr Lavender, that there is no better
fishermen on the coast. They are ferry fine, tall men ; and
they are ferry well dressed in their blue clothes ; and they
are manly fellows, whether they are drunk or whether they
are sober. Now look at this, sir, that in the worst of weather
they will neffer tek whisky with them when they go out to
the sea at night, for they think it is cowardly, and they are
ferry fine fellows and gentlemanly in their ways, and they
are ferry good-natured to strangers."

Further on he proceeds :—

" The trawling was not made legal then, and the men they
were just like teffles, with the swearing, and the drinking,
and the fighting that went on ; and if you went into the
harbour in the open day, you would find them drunk and
fighting, and some of them with blood on their faces, for it
wass a ferry wild time. It wass many a one will say that
the Tarbert men would run down the police boat some dark
night. And what wass the use of catching the trawlers now
and again, and taking their nets to be sold at Greenock,
when they would go themselves over to Greenock to the
auction and buy them back ? Oh, it was a great deal of
money they made then—I hef heard of a crew of eight men
getting £30 each man in the course of one night, and that
not seldom mirover."

" But why didn't the Government put it down ?" Lavender
asked.

" Well, you see," Mackenzie answered, with the air of a
man well acquainted with the difficulties of ruling, " you
see that it was not quite sure that the trawling did much
harm to the fishing.   And the " Jackal "—that wass the
Government steamer—she wass not much good in getting
the better of the Tarbert men, who are ferry good with their
boats in the rowing and ferry cunning whatever.   For the
buying boats they would go out to sea, and take the herring
there, and then the trawlers they would sink their nets and
come home in the morning as if they had not caught one
fish, although the boat would be white with the scales of the
herring.   And what is more, sir, the Government knew ferry
well that if trawling was put down then there would be a
ferry good many murders ; for the Tarbert men, when they
came home to drink whisky and wash the whisky down with
porter, they were ready to fight anybody."

So far as Lochfyne is concerned, trawling has
proved itself since being again legalised to be by
far the more remunerative mode of capture, and
the takes occasionally secured by this method are
enormous.   Only last season one crew, after summoning to its aid some half-a-dozen extra boats,
sent to market, as the result of one haul, about
350,000 herring, or one each for considerably more
than half of the entire population of Glasgow.

In the prosecution of fishing by this method, the
species of boat employed is a smart looking four-
oared skiff of about 25 feet keel and 9 feet beam,
carrying a jib and lug-sail.   From their upper wood-
work being simply varnished, they have a clean,
trig appearance, and their smartness is added to by
the great rake given to their masts in order that
the bottom of the boat may be as little cumbered

as possible. Their cost, when fully equipped with
mast, oars, sails, &c., is about £72, and many of
them are built in the boatbuilding yards of the
village.

Manned by a crew of four men, all of whom are
joint and equal owners, each boat is associated with
another in this mode of fishing, two boats being
necessary to the manipulation of one net. This
latter, which is, when made up, 170 yards long and
38 yards deep, is so shaped as to have a bag in the
centre at its deepest part. Along the top and the
bottom, the *back* and the *sole*, are attached ropes
which extend all round. Each end is further provided with a bridle of rope, to which are attached
those ropes which in working are used for drawing
the net towards the boats. The net is owned by
the crews of both boats, and costs usually, with
ropes, &c., £34. That the result of this equal
owning of property in net and boat is satisfactory
and works well there can be no doubt. Each man
receives an equal share in the earnings, and each
has equal stimulus to diligent and persevering effort.

The number of boats engaged in trawling, and
hailing from Tarbert, is 68, giving a total of 272
trawl fishermen. For the upkeep of the harbour
the very modest sum of one shilling and threepence
is paid to Stonefield annually by the owners of each
of these skiffs, while all boats above eight tons
burthen pay dues at the rate of one halfpenny per
ton register on every occasion they enter the harbour.

During the height of the fishing season, say in the month of July and August, when the harbour is well filled with boats of various kinds, and from various stations, it is a peculiarly interesting sight to watch the fleet setting out to sea on a fine afternoon, with just sufficient wind to waft them gently out of the bay, and into the broader waters of Lochfyne. Every few seconds a smack or skiff trims her sails, her rich brown wings, and glides silently through the rippling waters; no noise, no confusion, but a delightfully picturesque succession of ever-changing activity. Should the wind be defective, another scene is witnessed. Then each man has to bend to the oar, or, what is better, steam is pressed into service, and to the screw steamers engaged in buying the herring and carrying them to Glasgow may be seen attached a long tail of as many as a dozen skiffs, which are being conveniently and expeditiously towed out of the harbour, or, it may be, well on to the fishing ground.

> " A trawling skiff, a lively whiff,
>   Across the blue Lochfyne,
> And we will trust for sop and crust
>   To the depths of the driving brine.
>
> Oh who would lack a wholesome meal
>   When herring shoals are plenty?
> We'll fill the widow's humble creel,
>   And send the rich a dainty."

A curious life these fishermen lead, one which to them literally turns night into day. Off as a rule about three o'clock in the afternoon (earlier or later according to the distances they mean to go, and the nature of the wind), they may return anytime between midnight and next morning at breakfast time. Over the water they wander in search of their prey, listening for the *playing* of the herring in the dim twilight as they row gently along the shore. As darkness closes in their presence has to be discovered by other means. Then the sea glows with its strange uncanny light, and the waters seem alive in their scintillating beauty. Then every ripple causes a lambent gleam to shoot athwart the crests of the waves, every stroke of the oar produces its glowing eddy in the deep. As an old writer puts it, " the sea hath its stars no less than the sky," so the ocean possesses its light-bearing animals as does the land, and the fireflies of earth are paralleled by the light bearers of the sea, chief among them the little *Noctilucæ*—specks of living jelly, which exist in myriad in the waters of the ocean. Of great assistance is this phosphorescence, this lightening of the main, to the worker with the trawl, for through its influence much unnecessary work is avoided, no net being shot except where fish are seen to be. Up by the bow may be observed one of the crew rattling the anchor on the gunwale, and gazing intently while he watches for the rush of the startled herring through the burning waters, which become increasingly resplendent in the deepening darkness. The presence of herring being thus determined, and the nature of the ground permitting, the method of proceeding is as follows :—The companion boats approach one another and from that which contains the net the end of a rope, many fathoms in length, is handed to its consort. Should they commence to shoot the net from the shore, the latter remains stationary, while the other, either under sails or oars, proceeds to pay out the net in a semi-circle. If, on the other hand, they commence shooting from outside, the consort also moves round, but in the opposite direction. After the net is all into the water, it is followed by a rope, equal in length to that attached to the other end, and held by the consort. By this time the boats are within fifty yards of one another, and now an anchor, attached to the middle beam, is thrown out from each, and the men begin to pull in the ropes. And a long and a strong pull it often is, more particularly when the currents are rapid. After pulling in so far the anchors are lifted, the boats brought nearer, and the ropes drawn in as far as their attachments. Both ropes are now taken in charge by the crew of one boat, and quickly the two ends of the net are hauled in, while the consort passes round to the centre of the loop. If at all successful, as the net comes on board the herring are at first found sticking in the meshes, but as the centre is reached, where the bag is, they are seen, to the delight of the captors, in a greater or less heap

huddled closely together.   The consort now seizes
and supports the back-rope to prevent the fish
leaping out, while they are lifted into the bottom
of the boats with large baskets.   Soon the crews
may be knee deep in the most beautiful inhabitants
of the waters, for such in reality herring are when
freshly removed from their native element.   Their
brilliant silvery scales, shining in the dim light of
the stars, display a wealth of beauty impossible to
be witnessed but by the favoured fishers, for so
delicate is it that it vanishes, to a great extent, the
moment the hand touches it.   Should circumstances permit, a second and a third haul may be
attempted, and then comes the question of dispos-
ing of the fish.   The change which has occurred
within the last few years in connection with this
matter is a striking evidence of the enterprise of
the age.   Till within twelve years ago every herring
caught in the neighbourhood, with the exception
of a few sold to buying smacks at the fishing
ground, had to be taken in to Tarbert harbour,
where they were sold either for transporting by the
old " Mary Jane " or " Inverary Castle " to be disposed of as fresh herring late that night or next
day, or were retained at the quay or in vessels
in the bay in order to be cured.   Now all this is
changed, and seldom are any but a few herring
caught by drift nets disposed of in this way.   The
old bustle of Tarbert quay is gone; but it is well,
for a much more expeditious and convenient method

is now employed. Along with the fishing boats a
fleet of swift screw steamers, from six to sixteen in
number, proceed to sea each evening for the purpose of purchasing the herring as they are fished.
All night they go up and down the loch among the
trawlers, picking up some here and some there, as
fortune favours them, and, as morning approaches,
they set off for Glasgow at their utmost speed,
where they arrive often an hour before breakfast
time, returning to the fishing ground in time for
the next night's operations. The result of this
expedition is in many ways satisfactory. The
herring reach the table of the consumer in a much
fresher state than formerly—indeed, a person in
Glasgow may breakfast off herring that two or
three hours after he had gone to bed the night
before were sporting themselves in the waters of
Lochfyne; they may be sent to greater distances
in a fresh state, thus commanding a wider market,
and better prices fall to the fishermen.

How different all this must be to the conditions
which prevailed some centuries ago! Very early
in our history the herring fishing seems to have
been prosecuted on Lochfyne. In 1590, according
to Professor Cosmo Innes, Lochfyne herrings were
very highly appeciated in Scotland. He refers
also to a tennant of Breadalbane's, resident on the
shores of Lochfyne, having paid a portion of his
rent in herrings. But at a date much more
remote than this, according to the author of

" Glencreggan," Lochfyne came into prominence as a fishing centre.

" More than a thousand years ago," he says, " the fame of these Lochfyne herring had spread far beyond Tarbert and the adjacent coasts, for in the year 836 the Netherlanders came to Lochfyne to purchase the salted herrings. They were as cannie as the Scots, and they learnt the art and took up the trade of herring-curring. And they must have made the most of their knowledge as years went on, for in 1603 Sir Walter Raleigh speaks of the Dutch selling to other nations herrings that amounted in value to a million and a half of money, and, from first to last, employing two hundred thousand men in the herring trade, all these men being employed, and all these fish being caught on the coast of Scotland, and notably on Lochfyne."

From Pennant's " Tour in Scotland," published in 1770, we get an idea of some of the characteristics of the Lochfyne herring fishing in his day. He says :—

" Lochfyne is noted for the vast shoals of herrings that appear here in July and continue till January. The highest is from September to Christmas, when near six hundred boats, with four men in each, are employed. A chain of nets is used (for several are united) of a hundred fathoms, in length. As the herrings swim at very uncertain depths so the nets are sunk to the depth the shoal is found to take ; the success therefore depends much on the judgment or good fortune of the fishers in taking their due depths, for it often happens that one boat will take multitudes while the next does not catch a single fish, which makes the boatmen perpetually enquire of each other about the depth of their nets. These are kept up by buoys . . . . Sometimes the fish swim in twenty fathoms water, sometimes in forty, sometimes in fifty, and often times even at the bottom. It is computed that each boat gets about £40 in the season.

. . . . The present price is £1 4s. per barrel, but there is a drawback of the duty on salt for those that are exported.

The herring of Lochfyne are as uncertain in their migration as they are on the coast of Wales. They had for numbers of years quitted that water, but appeared again there within these dozen years. Such is the case with the lochs on all the western coast," &c., &c.

This description of course refers to drift-net fishing, trawling probably being unknown in these days.

Success in fishing is now, as in Pennant's days, a very uncertain quantity, and requires not a little faith for its successful prosecution. In fishing by trawl net it often appears especially so, for while some crews may have the good fortune of dividing on a Saturday sums yielding as much as ten, twenty, or even thirty pounds to each of eight men for their week's work, others may not have pocketed a pound for weeks together. Trusting, however, that their turn will come, and fortune smile on them as it usually does before the season has ended, they are ever encouraged to renewed and more persevering effort.

Saturday nights in the village, when all the fishermen are at home, and when all the earnings of the week are divided, are usually very busy, and when the local brass band turns out and promenades the street, or puts out to the "building" in the centre of the inner harbour for the purpose of charming the villagers from a distance, the scene is quite exhilarating, though it is unfortunately not

unfrequently marred by the diversion—or worse—
of some all too devoted worshippers of Bacchus,
who often find it a sore temptation to have too
much money in their pockets all at once.

The time of the year within which the fishing in
Lochfyne may be prosecuted is determined by Act
of Parliament, and extends from the beginning of
June till the end of January, but the close time is
not practically enforced.   Fishing is engaged in
whenever herring are to be got, which, however,
lately has not been before June, and not later than
November. When the fishing is over in Lochfyne,
some boats proceed to the North in order to fish in
the lochs there, but frequently they have been
compelled by the native fishermen, after serious
rows, to return home, the North men taking the
law into their own hands from their antipathy to
the use of the trawl net.   In the early months of
the year the majority of the men go south to the
Ballantrae and Girvan coasts, where it is understood is the spawning ground of the herring that
frequent Lochfyne.   Those who remain at home
generally engage in line fishing, both on Lochfyne
and West Loch Tarbert.

With but five nights' work in the week, and
frequent rests during stormy weather, and at the
height of the moon, when the herring are said to
seek the deeper parts of the loch, and when, at
anyrate, the nights are so clear that the assistance
of the phosphoresence in discovering their presence

is *nil,* the life of the Tarbert fisherman cannot be said to be a particularly hard one, more especially while the fishing continues in the neighbourhood, and he is enabled to get home each morning. He is wise enough to feed and clothe himself well while money is coming in and he can at all afford it, though he is also economical enough rather to pinch himself a bit than withdraw any of his savings from the bank once they have been lodged there. In early manhood and up to middle age he is robust and healthy, a man of broad shoulders, well-developed chest, fresh complexion, and, in many cases, very well featured. He cannot, however, be said to be long-lived. The exposure he endures, the spurts of hard work, and the quick cooling down in the cold night air seem to tell upon him speedily, and at a comparatively early age he loses his elasticity, begins to go down hill, and is forced to give up work. For a Tarbert fisherman to reach the age of seventy is quite an exceptional circumstance, and few grey heads are to be found in their midst.

It is somewhat astonishing to find how little is known regarding the habits of the herring, notwithstanding the thousands of men that have been engaged in their capture from time immemorial, and the source of wealth and food they have been to humanity. It is gratifying, however, to see that efforts are now being put forth by our Government and scientific bodies to dispel this ignorance, an d

by the establishment of aquariums in the neighbourhood of fishing stations and other convenient
situations, to study the conditions which favour
their development.   In a snug bay, called the
White Shore, at Tarbert, such an establishment
has been lately erected, and here, under the charge
of a superintendent and his assistants, much is
being done by artificial hatching and otherwise,
calculated to increase our knowledge in this direction, as well as to throw light on the special
characteristics of Lochfyne and its varied inhabitants.

CHAPTER X.

TALKS AND WALKS.

AS a pleasant spot to retire to for a time away from the worry and bustle of town life, Tarbert presents many inducements. Ever since the erection of the outer pier, but more particularly within the last twelve or fifteen years, during which time almost all the cottage accommodation now existing has been provided, the village has been speedily rising in favour with visitors to the seaside. With such a floating palace as the "Columba" at command—her popular and courteous officers, and her every convenience— it is not the serious matter it once was to reach the villages on the shores of Lochfyne. 'Tis but a five hours visit to an elegant drawing-room, a pleasant walk on a spacious promenade, where you rub shoulders often with the *elite* of the land, with travellers from every part of the world, and revel amid some of

nature's choicest scenes. Families who have grown
tired of the nearer towns and villages on the Firth
of Clyde, where everybody and his wife must now
strive to go year after year, and where the Glasgow
visitor often finds it hard to realise that he is out
of town at all, discover in such places as Tarbert
pleasant substitutes where they may have a thorough
change of air, of scene, and of society—retirement
with cheerfulness, life and activity without excitement.

Large enough to ensure most of the comforts of
civilization, Tarbert is still a village, presenting
many of the attractions of village life, both rural
and coast-like. To the artist tribe of mankind, who
flock hither in considerable numbers year after
year, it presents many inducements. In the bold
scenery of the eastern loch, with its snug creeks
shut in by jutting rocks covered with their golden
sea-weed; its island making the harbour the very
picture of security; its towering crag surmounted
by the old castle; its old thatched cottages that
still remain as relics of the past in the back street
and on the outskirts; and its enclosing hills giving
an aspect of compactness to the whole, they find
many a scene which it is their delight to pourtray.
Combined with these are also its attractions as a
centre of fishing life. The fishermen in their oil-
skins or comfortable blue clothes busily engaged in
preparations for sea, in mending nets, or in pulling
at the oar; the varied kinds of boats riding lazily

at anchor in the bay, or gliding out under sail impelled by the favouring breeze; a busy trawling scene, the boats well laden and the men bespattered plentifully with silvery scales; a morning on the quay among the herring; the nets hanging to dry in the breeze and sunshine, and reflected in the water along the margin of the bay ; or an old superannuated boat stranded on the sea-shore battered and bruised, all lend themselves to the pencil of the artist, while the scenes of softened beauty that characterise the hillsides of the western loch, contrive to place within a small compass such a variety of subjects as few places can afford.

Many a time and oft has the old castle, in the days of its decrepitude, been made to do duty on the canvas of the artist. Five hundred and sixty years of sunshine and of storm have told their tale of inevitable decay upon its structure; much of it has been demolished, but it is still picturesque in its ruin, and will well repay a visit. Since the fall of the stair some thirty years ago, its appearance has changed but little. Of the main building two well-built, massive walls, reaching apparently to their original height, and part of a third, still remain to testify to its general character. In form and extent it would appear to have ranked somewhere between the strong stately castles which reared their formidable towers in every part of the kingdom in the thirteenth century, and the peel or battlemented towers of the inferior barons—not so

extensive as the former, and more important than
the latter, as befitted a royal fortress.

If we consider the character of both of these, we
may be able to form an idea of what Tarbert Castle
was like in the days of its entirety. In the larger
castles, "the inner ward, called the donjon or keep,
was invariably the strongest part of the fortress,
and consisted of a large square tower, with walls
of tremendous thickness, situated in the centre of
the other buildings, from which, however, it was
usually detached. The lower storey was employed
as a dungeon for the prisoners and a receptacle for
the stores; the second floor contained the guard-
rooms for the garrison; and on the third were the
great hall and other apartments, which formed the
residence of the baron or castellan and his family.
In the uppermost rooms were deposited the warlike
engines required for the defence of the castle during
a siege. For the sake of security, the principal
entrance to the keep was generally placed pretty
far up the wall, and was protected by a strong
gate of thick oak with iron knobs, a portcullis or
grating usually composed of iron, and a drawbridge.
The other defences consisted of one or two strong
exterior walls with flanking towers; and beyond
the outer wall was a broad breast-work or barbican,
and a moat which encircled the whole building."

The peel, on the other hand, was a "large square
battlemented tower, protected by an outer wall and
some light fortifications. The walls of these forta-

lices, however, were of immense thickness, and, as the rooms were vaulted, and each storey formed a separate lodgment, they were capable of making a considerable resistance to an enemy. But their greatest security was afforded by their situation, which was commonly on a precipice, or on the banks of a torrent, or in the midst of almost impassable morasses."

The square tower of Tarbert Castle consisted of four storeys, which reach at present to a height of forty-eight feet at the south-east corner. It was built of whinstone, with a coping of red sandstone forming massive projecting mouldings. From north to south it measures forty-one feet, and from east to west twenty-six feet. In the lower flat, and stretching the whole length within the walls from north to south, is a vaulted chamber popularly called the dungeon, which, from its dark gruesome character, is seldom explored, and which is much more extensive than it is generally supposed to be. In length it measures twenty-six feet, while its breadth is thirteen feet. Its height to the spring of the arch is not less than six feet six inches, and to its centre ten feet. At the further end is a recess four feet six inches broad, and reaching six feet into the southern wall. Extending through the remainder of this wall is a shot hole three feet long, which shows the total thickness of the wall at this part to be nine feet. In the walls of either side of this recess is another recess of a similar character, but of much smaller dimensions. In its northern wall, which is here six feet in thickness, a second shot hole is seen, showing that this rather ample prison house was also used in time of need for assisting in the defence. Its masonry is of a very superior character, and the prisoner who should attempt to make his escape would have found himself very effectually baffled. Its entrance and much of its exterior are now blocked with fallen mason work. From the flat above, on which was the main entrance which is said to have opened on the west side, there is evidence of its having been reached by an internal stair, while on the east side it was entered from the ground level, through a door close to the north corner. Before reaching this door from the outside, it is necessary to pass through some subsidiary buildings, which, however, bear evidence of having been erected at a later date than the tower. These buildings are simply set up against the latter without being *tied* to it in any way, and are of very inferior workmanship, being built of very small stones with poor lime. That they did not form part of the original structure is further borne out by the fact of there being a shot-hole in the north wall of the tower at a point where it could not possibly be of use after these parts were built.

It is possible they constitute a portion of the structures erected by James IV. during his visit in 1494. Though built of inferior material, they are of considerable thickness, being seven feet in many places. From east to west they measure twenty-nine feet, and from north to south twenty-four feet, with a height of about twenty feet.

The second storey of the tower is marked by a large window in an arched recess on its southern side, as well as by several smaller windows and loop-holes. The third storey is indicated by a handsome arched window, from the side of which a passage in the wall runs along to the south side, giving access to several loop-holes. In the fourth flat there are several windows and loop-holes, with a very large fire-place on the northern side, the chimney leading from which passes through the pointed part of the north gable.

No trace remains of the moat, but the outworks —the round towers and the walls—are still clearly marked, showing them to have covered a large extent of ground. Towards the north and east the remains of several round towers, and of a wall on the edge of the more precipitous part of the crag, are well seen. Two of these towers on the east measure twenty-seven feet in diameter, while their walls are seven feet in thickness. On the west the remains of two towers of a similar character exist, whilst on this side also a large area one hundred and twenty-six feet by one hundred and ten feet, still popularly called the *barracks*, is surrounded by the remains of high walls, which enclose the foundations of structures the nature of which it is now impossible to determine.

In connection with the supplying of the castle with water, a common tradition, though a very unlikely one, exists in the village, that it was led from the Knapdale side in pipes under the harbour, through a large sub-marine passage, and the following story, common to a good many places, is often told relative to this passage:—At a date, variously stated, a certain person of a bold turn of mind determined to explore this unknown region, and for this purpose entered it at a spot marked by a large separated rock, under which the entrance is supposed to be. This spot is known by the name of *Uarrih Mac Ruari.* For companionship he took with him his faithful dog, and, possibly in the hope of scaring the powers of evil, he furnished himself also with a pair of bagpipes. For a considerable time he was heard playing a tune which the listeners interpreted as a defiance to the fairies or other beings of an inferior order who opposed his progress, but after a time all sounds ceased, and neither man nor dog was ever seen again.

It is not a little sad to see this old royal fortress —royal in its origin, and on several occasions the abode of royalty—being allowed to fall further into ruin without the slighest effort being made to assist it in baffling the forces of decay. Much might be done by some large-hearted and patriotic individuals to help in preserving what still remains

of a structure at once so interesting and so picturesque, as well as in improving the precincts and
rendering them somewhat more attractive to the
lover of the relics of other and stormier days.

Should the visitor happen to be of an enquiring
turn of mind, and come across some of the more
communicative of the inhabitants, he will have
little difficulty in extracting from them some old
stories associated with the district. Here are a
few :—Early in the present century the old predatory habits of the Highlanders were still strong
among the inhabitants of this district, and sheep
stealing, which was looked upon rather as a justifi-
able action than as a case of ordinary theft, was
very common among them. On one occasion the
house of a person who was very seriously suspected
of a crime of this nature was, with little delay, and
while the sheep was yet uncut, visited by a band
of searchers. Having received a moment or two's
notice, which, however, was not sufficient to allow
the delinquent to remove the carcase from the
house, he hit upon a novel method of deceiving his
visitors. Snatching up the sheep, he, with considerable presence of mind, placed it in a child's
cradle, and set himself to rock it with great earnest-
ness, crooning all the time a Gaelic lullaby. The
device was eminently successful. Not looking
very closely at the cradle, and never dreaming but
that it simply contained its usual occupant, the

searchers departed without discovering the object of their visit.

While Lord Colonsay was at the bar, a Tarbert woman then resident in Glasgow was accused of the murder of her husband. This eminent lawyer, who had an interest in the district around Tarbert from the fact of his maternal grandfather having been the Laird of Dunmore, undertook her defence, and succeeded in breaking down the case for the prosecution completely. After the conclusion of the trial, the Tarbert minister, who had been present in court, hurried up to Lord Colonsay, and remonstrated with him on the impropriety of securing the acquittal of one whom the clergyman regarded as a guilty woman. To which Lord Colonsay very quietly and very effectively replied, "Go home to your charge; I have saved that woman's life in this world, it is your duty to see that it is saved in the next."

A circumstance not a little interesting is the late date at which the mole found its way into Kintyre. Not till a few years previous to 1843 had it crossed the isthmus of Tarbert, but it had gradually made its way southward, reaching in the above year a point 18 miles from Tarbert. It is somewhat peculiar to find that its non-appearance in the peninsula had been associated in the Highland mind with the presence of the clan Campbell. According to tradition and prophecy, the moles on their arrival were to drive the Campbells before

them and take possession of their estates, and when
the moles got the length of the Mull, not a Campbell, it was anticipated, would remain throughout
the length and breadth of Kintyre. So they said,
but Kintyre is now over-run by moles, but without
effecting any sensible decrease in the numbers of
that ubiquitous clan.

We have given in a previous chapter some historical references regarding the introduction of the
Campbells into Kintyre. The following story is
told in connection with the manner in which the
M'Callums first came into the district:—A tenant
farmer named Callum, resident somewhere in the
North, had twelve sons, all of whom were fine
strapping fellows. On a certain New-Year's-Day
they all appeared dressed in their best at a grand
feast given by the great lord of the place. It so
happened that this lord's lady was childless, and
when she saw Callum's handsome sons she envied
him. This was bad news to Callum, and he felt
persuaded that some mischief must befall them,
from the lady's envious eye. And so it did. One
by one they fell sick and slipped away, without
any apparent disease, till by next New-Year's-Day
only three remained. In despair, Callum advised
these to go and leave the place, and escape from
the influence of the evil eye. They obeyed. Each
took a horse, put their baggage into creels slung
across their horses' backs by *woodies* or twisted
rods, and set off they knew not whither, but by

their father's advice, they were to go on till their woodies broke. When they reached Kilmartin, the woodies on the first horse gave way, and here the rider settled.

The other two set off, crossed the isthmus of Tarbert, and entered Kintyre. When they reached Clachan the woodies on another horse broke, and the third brother had to proceed on his solitary way alone. On he tramped till he almost feared he would be forced to march into the sea. By the time, however, he reached Southend, the woodies broke; all got comfortably settled, Callum saved his three sons, and cheated the envious eye. Each of these sons had large families, and in process of time they became numerous. On one occasion those of Kintyre agreed to salute their brethren of Kilmartin, and despatched a message requesting these latter to meet them half-way, which they agreed to do. Both parties started at the appointed time, and met near Tarbert, but did not know one another. Then they demanded each other's names, but in those days it was considered a sign of cowardice to answer such a question when put in such a manner. So, without further ado, they fell fiercely on each other, and fought long and hotly till most of both parties were slain. At last, however, after all this mischief was done, they came to understand the mistake, when those that remained alive cordially shook hands, and expressed their great sorrow at what had been done. They then buried their dead brethren, and returned again to their own homes. Such was the manner in which the friendship of the M'Callums was lovingly cemented.

This story recalls one of the numerous traditions which exist regarding Bruce in connection with his wanderings in Kintyre. After leaving Sliabh Ghaoil, where he had been protected and fed by the goat, he passed into Kintyre. After proceeding some miles, he met in a lonesome spot a man whose name he demanded to know. Neither, however, would tell to the other his name, and forthwith they drew their swords and fell a-fighting. Till exhausted they fought desperately, and then rested. After taking fresh breath they set to again, and once more they had to give up quite exhausted, neither of them having got the advantage. Then said the king, "This is pitiful work that we give ourselves, alone and in this dreary place. It will answer no good end, even if we should kill each other. Tell me your name, and I will tell you mine." "Agreed," replied the stranger. "I am Robert Bruce," said the king. "And I," replied his adversary, "am General Douglas." The latter, the good Lord Douglas, was one of Bruce's stoutest friends, and, like the king, was in disguise and a fugitive. Instantly they threw aside their swords and embraced each other affectionately, proceeding afterwards on their way together.

Less than half a century ago the belief in witchcraft was still prevalent in Tarbert, and it was somewhat strengthened by an incident which is said to have occurred in the neighbourhood about that time. One night a Tarbert person observed a hare on the path in front of him, which he suspected to be in reality a witch which had taken that form. Having a fowling piece in his hand, he quickly loaded it with a small silver coin (the only effective metal in such circumstances), and fired, wounding the hare in one eye. The next morning, sure enough, it was discovered that a woman in the village had a fresh wound in the corresponding eye. This rendered the Tarbert people certain that they had a witch in their midst, and they openly reproached the woman about it. Her reply took the form of a fierce assertion to the effect that the marksman had been ready enough with the gun, but that he would soon be shot himself. By and by, it did happen as she stated, the man dying from the effects of a gun shot wound, but whether accidentally or intentionally inflicted could never be determined.

Not the least of Tarbert's attractions is the freedom to roam over hill and dale without the dread of over-zealous gamekeepers or annoying prosecutions—a boon which can only be fully appreciated by the lover of nature who has had the experience in some less favoured spot of being confined to the hard and dusty highway through the selfish caprice of some despicable territorial magnate, who is more concerned about a few brace of grouse than about the welfare or esteem of his less fortunate fellow creatures. A climb of a few hundred feet to the top of Roebuck Hill, on the north side of the village, rewards the wanderer with a wide and varied prospect. As he looks back, on gaining the summit, he obtains a bird's eye view of the village lying cosily at the foot of the hill. To the left is the wide expanse of Lochfyne, stretching northwards before him as far as the granite quarries of Crarae, and opening towards the south into the Firth of Clyde. The Ayrshire coast, Bute, Inchmarnock, the Skate Island, the Cowal coast from Ardlamont to Otter, Lochgilphead, and the green peninsula of Barmore, all lie before him as in a picture; while to the west the isthmus, with its hamlets of Laglune and Cairnbaan, and further along that of West Tarbert; the western loch, beautifully wooded on either side, and dotted with an occasional island; and, on a fine day, far in the distance the coast of Antrim, add to the beauty and expansiveness of the view.

Driving or walking in the neighbourhood of the village is very enjoyable. By the Ardrishaig road, which rises very abruptly, you quickly obtain a considerable altitude, from which you look down on the harbour and the broad expanse of Lochfyne stretching away towards the south. Proceeding, you pass by and through considerable plantations (which, however, have been sadly thinned by the

storms of a late winter), leaving on the left the
farm house of Ashens, and on the right the stead-
ing of Stonefield home farm. A little further
along, through a break in the wood, Stonefield
House is seen, beautifully situated among its trees.
As you proceed—which you will probably be
tempted to do very slowly if you are at all a
lover of Nature, if you can be wooed from the
straight road by the music of innumerable birds,
by the busy sight of a colony of ants hard at work
upon some decaying stump, or by the desire to
hunt for delicate ferns and more delicate mosses—
you approach again the shore, obtaining an effective
view of Barmore peninsula as it stretches out into
the loch by which it is so nearly severed from the
mainland. From this point onwards to Ardrishaig
the road winds along by the side of Lochfyne,
which reaches grandly away to the right, while it
is lined on the left by the beautiful hillsides,
covered on their lower levels by fresh hazel brushwood and young copsewood. The rock and shore
scenery is here very fine. At a distance of about
six miles from Tarbert, Erin's House, a white
castellated-looking building, is passed, and as you
approach nearer Ardrishaig you discover an occasional stream traversing with soothing cadence
over its pebbly bottom, or rushing headlong,
grumbling and growling, through its beautiful glen
and over its rocky bed.

A pleasant little walk of about four miles is

that through Glenralloch and round the base of
Roebuck Hill. Taking the Ardrishaig road for
about a mile and a quarter, you come to a point
where it joins another running at right angles to it.
Holding by your left you strike into Glenralloch.

After proceeding uphill for a couple of hundred yards, you come in sight both of Lochfyne
and West Loch Tarbert, the latter on a bright day
lying before you like a sheet of silver in the
brilliant noonday. On both hands the hillsides
are lovely, and as the glen opens out towards the
loch, you approach on either hand cultivated fields,
and, on the right, on a little eminence, the farm
house of Glenralloch, comfortably situated among
its trees. As the road comes near the water, it
strikes across the head of the loch, passing on the
left Glenakil House and the prominent hill of that
name, and joins the Campbeltown road, which it
meets at right angles on the isthmus. In Glenakil
there was an ancient burying ground, which, since
the formation of the Tarbert one, has been disused.
Regarding it an old story is told. About the early
part of last century a family, who farmed the
adjoining ground, thinking they might make use
of the burying-ground and include it in their farm,
demolished the wall and removed the tombstones
in order that they might not interfere with their
ploughing operations, &c. This family comprised
seven sturdy brothers, all of whom, so runs the
story, soon took to a reckless mode of living, went

from bad to worse, and died shortly afterwards—a manifest judgment for their sacrilege.

Rambles by the West Loch! Either side is worthy of an excursion. Suppose you have a walk to Dunmore, upon the northern side. Crossing the isthmus, with its hamlets of Laglune and Cairnbaan, and passing round by the head of the loch, you traverse a pleasant road running along the side of the water, and lined with a variety of copsewood. Up there, on the right, is the home of the royal fern, the monarch of its tribe. Presently you reach a fine stream called Abhuin-nan-Ghillean (the youths' river), which tumbles down its shady glen and rushes towards the sea, after having parted with some of its power in the shape of a lade, which is utilized for driving a saw-mill hard by. The following story is told regarding the origin of the river's name:—On a certain occasion five brothers were journeying on foot along the shores of the West Loch. On their way they were met by on old woman, who was noted for the power of her evil wishes. Having probably displeased her in some way, she rather ungraciously informed them that they would never reach the end of their journey; and, accordingly, as they were crossing this stream, which was not then bridged over, they one after another slipped from the stepping stones into the rushing water and were drowned.

We are now on the Kintarbert estate, the property of John Neill Macleod, Esq., to whom it was bequeathed, along with the Saddell estate, by the late Miss M'Neill-Campbell. On the hill is an unostentatious-looking house, used as a shooting lodge. Beyond Abhuin-nan-Ghillean the road strikes up hill, winding by the side of the stream, the banks of which are well wooded, and soon you are high above the loch, among the hills, and on the solitary moorland. After passing a house or two and some cultivated patches which have been snatched from nature and reclaimed, the road again winds down to the loch, crossing, at the foot of the hill, another considerable stream. The road is now comparatively level, and easily traversed. On the opposite side the hills of Kintyre stand boldly out in their varied shades of living green. Forward a couple of miles and you come to a gentleman's residence glorying in the unpronounceable name of Achaglachgach. On both sides the road is bordered with lovely copses of mountain ash, of dwarfy saugh, of hardy oak, of lively birch, and kindly hazel, while the bramble thrusts its straggling presence into the choicest company, and binds them all in one. On the right the hills are finely wooded to the top. Presently Dunmore House, an old renovated keep, the residence of Miss Campbell, comes in sight, nestling cosily among its trees. You are now eight miles from Tarbert, and probably thinking it high time to retrace your steps, determining some other fine day to make the

acquaintance of the other side of the loch, and
hoping to derive an equal amount of pleasure. And
probably you will. The road to Campbeltown,
more particularly the first six miles of it, is of ever-
changing interest. It is one of those roads which
owe their power of pleasing to minute, delicate, and
refined beauties, the scenery of which must be
waited upon and courted in order to be thoroughly
appreciated. Hence the greater pleasure derived
in walking, and being admitted into closer fellow-
ship with nature. After passing the hamlet of
West Tarbert, where in days gone by considerable
quantities of whisky were distilled, the road skirts
the water on the right hand, while on the left the
hills, clad in tangled brushwood interspersed with
varied pines, rise abruptly up from its very side,
displaying many little scenes of winsome beauty. At
a distance of two and a half miles from East Tarbert
Pier is that of West Tarbert, from which daily communication with Islay is maintained. The distance
between the two piers is traversed by coaches, which
convey both passengers and luggage in time for joining the Islay steamer or the " Columba." Opposite
the pier is the hamlet of Abhuin-nan-Ghillean,
with its green point stretching far out into the loch.
Half-a-mile further on is Escart Bay, sheltered
by its island, Eilean-da-Ghallagan, on which
until quite recently were the ruins of what was
variously considered a hermit's cell and a fort, said
to have been occupied by Allan-nan-Sop. It is

almost unmarked now, the stones having been removed by the Gigha fishermen from time to time as ballast. To the left of the road, and pleasantly situated on an eminence, is Escart House, presently occupied by Neil Sinclair, Esq. As you proceed, Corranbuie, Sunnyside, Dippin, and Woodhouse are successively passed as the road strikes more inland among trees and cultivated patches. At a distance of three and a half miles from the village is the house of Rhu, an old residence of the younger Stonefields. The plantations hereabouts are very extensive, reaching for miles together almost without a break, while many a shady nook and wimpling burn invite the wayfarer from the beaten track to wander along its bank, or rest and enjoy the poetry of nature. Another mile and you approach the bay of Kennacraig, where the road turns off to the left, and you come in sight of that which leads to Skipness, cutting over the hills and right across the country to the other side of Kintyre. On the left of the road, and right above the bay, is the old burying place of Cladh Bhride, where lie buried some members of the Stonefield family. Following the straight road, and leaving the Skipness one on your left, a walk of a mile on an elevated plateau, past picturesque old houses and piles of sable peat, brings you to where you descend on Whitehouse, a snug little village, having its post office, schoolhouse, blacksmith's shop, &c. Like most country hamlets, it has its stream, which drives a saw-mill and a pretty little stream it is, as it ripples away towards the sea. From this point onwards, as far as Clachan, a distance of five miles, the road is extremely hilly, giving some fine glimpses of the loch as you pass along. Campbeltown is yet some twenty-seven miles away, but if the traveller is desirous of visiting the town of distilleries he may join the three-horse coach which daily makes the double journey between it and Tarbert, a distance in all of seventy-six miles.

West Loch Tarbert, around which we have been rambling, is an arm of the sea nine miles in length, stretching up between the mainland and the peninsula of Kintyre. Though not of large extent, it is romantically pretty—a smaller Loch Katrine—displaying a soft beauty which contrasts pleasantly with the barer and bolder scenery of its eastern sister. An amphitheatre of hills, covered with trees of varied shades, cultivated and fresh green patches along the lower levels, and here and there a crofter's cottage or gentleman's mansion house, gratify the eye on either side. Standing out in the distance, boldly against the sky, is the hill of Dunskeig, which commands the entrance to the loch, and which is so admirably adapted by nature for a place of defence. On its summit it bears both a vitrified and a circular fort. An occasional island here and there in the loch serves to break up the monotony of the water, and adds to the picturesqueness of the scene. Here is Maculloch's description, which may

be taken as a just one, though the loch seems not
to be on a large enough scale for him to apply to it
the epithet of picturesque:—

" The navigation of Loch Tarbert is exceedingly beautiful,
without being strictly picturesque. The ground is neither
high nor bold ; but the shores are varied in form and character, often beautifully wooded, and in many places highly
cultivated ; while a considerable rural population, and some
houses of more show and note, give it that dressed and
civilised air which is by no means an usual feature in the
shores of the Highlands. , . . . I know not what
Loch Tarbert may be at other times, but when I made its
circuit, it was with sun-rise on one of the loveliest mornings
of June. The water was like a mirror ; and as the sun
reached the dewy birchwoods, the air was perfumed by their
fragrance, while the warbling of ten thousand thrushes on
all sides, with the tinkling sound of the little waves that
curled on the shore, and the gentle whispering of the morning air among the trees, rendered it a perfect scene of
enchantment."

> " Art dulled wi' grief ? gae seek relief
>   Where nae sound heart can harbour't ;
> And stray or ride on ilka side
>   O' pleasant West Loch Tarbert.
>
> The wind that shakes the hazel brakes,
>   And fans the weary reaper,
> Shall saftly clear frae blinding tear
>   The eyelids of the weeper."

Hugh M'Lean, in his poem of " MacCalein's
Raid," thus speaks of the loch as seen from the
summit of one of the neighbouring hills. After
referring to Islay and Jura, he proceeds:—

> " But from that level lower your searching glance,
>   See West Loch Tarbert from the deep advance,
>   Worming an inland path, which nature decks,
>   Until its dark-brown glass, below, reflects
>   The motley mountain shades and wooded land,
>   Which fringe its jutting points on every hand."

A circumstance which usually strikes the visitor is the difference between the tides in the two lochs. You may just have left East Tarbert with the tide full in, and after a walk of some ten minutes come in sight of the West Loch, only to find it ebb water. The fact is, that while the East Loch follows the usual rule of two tides in twenty-four hours, the West Loch may have four or five in the same space of time; or, on the other hand, in stormy weather, the tide may remain in for days together, circumstances which seem to be due to its more direct connection with the Atlantic.

This irregularity, we learn from the following extract from "Pennant's Tour," was noted by James Watt when he visited the neighbourhood:—

" According to some remarks Mr James Watt, of Glasgow, favoured me with, the spring tides in East Tarbat flow ten feet six inches ; in West Tarbat only four feet six inches, or in very extraordinary tides two feet higher. The tides in the West Loch are most irregular ; sometimes neither ebb nor flow ; at other times ebb and flow twice in a tide, and the quantity of the false ebb is about one foot. The mean height of the Firth of Clyde is greater than that of West Tarbat."

An incident in connection with the old Tarbert

packet and the notorious pirate, Paul Jones, is thus referred to by Cuthbert Bede:—

"In 1778, Paul Jones, the pirate, attacked the Tarbert Packet and plundered it. Major Campbell, of Islay, was on board of her, with a large fortune of gold and valuables acquired in India, from whence he was returning to end his days in Islay ; and he had safely reached the Sound of Islay, and was close to home, when the pirate attacked the vessel, and robbed Major Campbell of all his property."

In 1825 a new quay was erected for the convenience of the packet, and the general trade of the Islands.

Within the last four years (1882) the long contemplated project of connecting the waters of East Loch Tarbert with those of the Western Loch by means of a canal has been again revived, only, however, apparently to collapse, after the manner of former schemes instituted for a similar end. The difficulties and dangers encountered in connection with rounding the Mull of Kintyre, the storms which sport themselves around that dreaded promontory, aggravated as they are by the violent tides which come sweeping down from the Minch, and in from the Western Ocean, the fogs which love to linger there when all the surrounding neighbourhood is clear, together with the delay due to these circumstances and the long round about voyage necessary to gain the Western and Northern Islands from the Clyde, all combined to enforce the desirableness of securing a route which should be to a great extent free from such dangers and delays. The comparative ease with which a canal could be cut between East and West Loch Tarbert (the highest point of the isthmus being only 47 feet above the sea) has long pointed it out as the position best suited for such an undertaking, and in the year 1771, ere the Crinan Canal was commenced, the isthmus was surveyed by the celebrated engineer, James Watt, as an alternative route. His estimate for a channel 16 feet deep was about £120,000. The difficulties which then prevailed, particularly as to sailing ships beating in the narrow channel of West Loch Tarbert, led to the adoption of the Crinan Canal. Henry Bell having by his genius removed these difficulties by the introduction of steam vessels, the idea became more practicable, and in the year 1828 this ever active planner and legitimate successor of Watt paid a visit to the district for the purpose of making a survey of it. It was the last scheme which he developed, and its main points may be gathered from the following letter which he addressed to the more important individuals of Argyllshire from his death-bed two years afterwards.:—

"Helensburgh, 23rd August, 1830.

"TO THE GENTLEMEN, FREEHOLDERS, AND MERCHANTS OF ARGYLESHIRE.

"Gentlemen,—I beg to submit to you what I humbly conceive would be a great improvement in the means of communication in the County of Argyll ; such an improvement, I believe, as would add greatly to the value of the

western isles of that shire, and to the counties adjacent. As
I have long been convinced that a canal, running across that
neck of land between east and west Tarbert, would present
an expeditious and safe means of communication for vessels
passing from the Clyde to the western coast of Scotland, I
took a careful survey of the ground two years ago, and found
my scheme perfectly practicable.

" I have latterly consulted several persons conversant with
the excavating of canals, and my estimate of the straight cut
which I have planned out, and desire to submit to your
inspection, is, if cut 50 feet wide at bottom, and 60 at top,
and 3 feet deep

Below low water, cost - - - -	£37,000
And if 6 feet below low water, - -	23,000
And if 9 feet, add - - - -	30,000
Total expense, - - - -	£90,000

Depth at high water mark of these several cuts, as follows :
—First, 15 feet ; second, 18 feet ; third, 21 feet ; the former
affording passage for the generality of vessels trading to and
from the river Clyde.

" This canal would form a very splendid opening, almost
unequalled for grandeur and sublimity. There would be no
impediment whatever to the navigation in this cut, it being
made in a straight line, through solid rock, without locks or
draw-bridges. It would certainly form one of the grandest
openings in Europe ; but its utility would be incomparably
more important than its rural magnificence and fascinating
beauty, attractive as these would be.

" The first cost would be all that is required for many
years to come. There are, indeed, two bridges required ;
but from the nature of the ground, they could be placed so
high as to allow vessels to pass under the arches in full sail.
The span of these arches to be 70 feet, the breadth 25 feet,
and built of stone, of which there is plenty at hand.

" The money query is, How is this great projected undertaking to be effected ? I answer, by a joint stock company
—of 100 shares each. The proprietors of those islands, who

will be chiefly benefitted, will find it their interest not to discourage or lose sight of the scheme, though they should be staggered at first by the amount of the expense to carry it into execution. A second query is, What interest are we to expect for the outlay of hard cash, and from what source, or sources, is it to arise ? It will be from vessels passing to and from the western coast of Scotland, and the north of Ireland. Merchant vessels, too, from America and the West Indies, may be expected to take advantage of this cut. In my opinion the charge on these vessels would be as follows, and which would produce a considerable sum to the proprietors :—

Small rowing boats, each,	-	-	£0	2	6
Half-decked fishing wherries, each,			0	5	0
Vessels from 10 to 50 tons, per ton,			0	1	0
Do.,	50 to 100 tons, do.,		0	0	9
Do.,	100 upwards, do.,		0	0	6

These charges, I presume, would amply repay the shareholders for their outlay ; as, after the first year's opening there would be a dividend each year to a certainty, as no after expenses would be incurred but the collector's fees. If these hints of mine, for the benefit of the commerce of my country, and especially of the shire in whose prosperity you are more immediately concerned, should be approved of by you, and should issue in your taking the steps necessary for the completion of the scheme, I shall consider my exertions in the business well rewarded. I remain, Gentlemen, your most obedient servant,

(Signed)   " HENRY BELL."

Fifteen years after the above date a decided advance was made towards the construction of this desiderated waterway. The defects of the Crinan Canal, with its seventeen narrow locks, were becoming more and more apparent, and in the year 1845 a company was formed with a capital of

£150,000, for the cutting of a channel 56 feet wide and 18 feet deep. The necessary Act of Parliament was duly secured, and such was the esteem in which the undertaking was held that shares amounting to four times the capital desired were applied for. " Various causes, particularly the monetary crisis of 1847, prevented the company proceeding with the works; and negotiations took place between the Government and the directors, resulting in an arraugement under which the company was to abandon their Act, and the canal was to be formed by the Government." After a minute inspection and favourable report by Captain Sir E. Belcher and Lieutenant-Colonel Yule, a bill authorising the transfer of the undertaking to Government was introduced by the Chancellor of the Exchequer late in the session of 1847, but obstacles were raised to its passing, and the arrangement fell through. The dissolution of the company followed in 1849.

From the above date till the year 1882 the project slept, but in the latter year it was revived, and a provisional committee of influential gentlemen, headed by his Grace the Duke of Argyll, was formed. This committee in the following year applied for and obtained an Act of Parliament empowering them to undertake the proposed work, the estimated cost of which was £178,400 sterling. It was proposed that the share capital should be £200,000; that a channel not less than 75 feet in width, with a depth at mean water of not less than 20 feet, should be cut between the lochs (the total length from loch to loch along the line of the canal being 1630 yards) ; that a path 10 feet wide should be formed along one side ; that a single lock between high and low water mark should be constructed in East Loch Tarbert for the purpose of preventing any interruption to the traffic from the tidal currents ; and that the harbours of both the East and West Lochs should be so improved as to fit them for the consequent increased traffic. " Upon a moderate calculation " it was estimated by the promoters that the canal would be so taken advantage of by steam and sailing vessels to and from the Western Isles, Norway, &c., as to yield an annual return of £11,750.

That such sanguine expectations would be realized was seriously doubted by many well able to form an opinion, and from the fact that, after a period of nearly three years from the passing of the Act of Parliament, nothing is now heard of the scheme, we may infer that the doubt was largely shared in by the monied members of the community. That the canal, however, would be extensively taken advantage of, and that the trade with the west and north would be very consider- ably increased as the result of the more direct, safe, and expeditious route, admits of no doubt, whilst we may well believe that the enterprise of the age would be employed in providing communication for the "tourist race" by what would be a most delightful way of reaching "Oban and the North." The necessity for conveying boats across the isthmus, as is still done, would then have ceased, and Kintyre would in reality be an island, as Magnus Barefoot so long ago endeavoured by stratagem to make it.

What the influence of such a canal would be on the future of Tarbert, it would be difficult to determine. While changing its appearance very considerably, it would doubtless improve its harbour, and probably lead to the increased prosperity of the inhabitants.

That some such improvement as would be effected in such a case in the sanitary condition of the harbour is necessary, is only too apparent, both to the visual and olfactory organs, and it is to be hoped that in connection with the new water and drainage scheme, the community will see it to be both to their comfort and ultimate profit to proceed in a thorough manner with the cleaning out and deepening of the inner harbour, and thus add not a little to the amenities of their otherwise attractive village.

GLOSSARY.

Abaysit—humbled
Addettit—indebted
Allayne—alone
Apon—upon
Attoure—moreover
Awin—own

Bak—back
Befoir—before
Bodin—equipped
Bot—but
Brodyr—brother
Bruikit but—possessed without

Cair—care
Centrical—central
Counsale—council
Couth—could
Croce—cross
Cum—come

Darloch—a short sword
Dewlie—duly
Drawand—drawing

Eftir—after
Evident—a title deed

Falt—want
Far—journey
Fayr—go
Feir of weir—prepared for war
Flote—afloat
Forasmekle—forasmuch
Fra—from
Frehalder—freeholder

Ga—go
Geir—gear
Gert—made to
Gif—if
Guidis—goods

Hacquetbutis—a kind of musket
Haif—have
Haill—whole
Havershon (habergeon)—a cuirass or cot of mail
Hes—has
Hey—high
Hienes—highness
Horning—denouncing as a rebel

Impetrat—warrant
Indorsat—endorsed

Lykeways—likewise

Maich—son-in-law
Maid—made
Maist—most
Males—rent or feu-duty
Mar—more
Mastis—masts
Materis—matters
Menye—followers
Mercatt—market

Noblay—nobility

Onywyse—anyways
Owtakyn—excepting

Pane—pain
Pepill—people

Quhen—when
Quhilk—which

Rapys—ropes
Retourit—return of value of
        lands

Sait—seat
Samin—same
Scarslie—scarcely

Schipp—ship
Schiref—sheriff
Se—sea
Sesing—sasine
Seys—seas
Sick—such
Sone—soon
Spek—speak
Stented—taxed
Sua—his
Suld—should
Swa—so

Ta—to
Tey—tie
Thai—they
Thar—there
Thir—these
Throw—through
Toppis—tops
Tuk—took
Twa—two
Tyme—time

Utheris—others

Wald—would
Weill—well
Weir—war
Wynd—wind
Wyne—win
Wyst—knew

'East Tarbert, Cantire'
A woodcut reproduced from *Glencreggan: or, A Highland Home in Cantire* by Cuthbert Bede (London, 1861), illustrated by the author. Bede describes Tarbert as 'The capital of Herringdom'.